# AN ELEGANT LION NAMED GEORGE

A LIVING LION DOLL THAT IS AN
ASSISTANT TO A VETERAN OF
VEHICULAR HOMICIDE? AMAZING!

Ingram Content Group
One Ingram Blvd.
La Vergne, TN 37086
www.ingramspark.com

Printed in the United States of America

First Printing, 2020

ISBN 978-1-952740-17-6 (Hardback)
ISBN 978-1-952740-16-9 (Paperback)
ISBN 978-1-952740-15-2 (EPUB)

mkrautant.com
mitchellkrautant@gmail.com

# TABLE OF CONTENTS

# CHAPTER 1

## ABOUT GEORGE THE LION AND HIS CARE FOR A VETERAN

George is the name of the Lion Doll that saved my life. I don't know how he got that name. I think he got it from my roommate who brought him to the hospital I was in when I was recovering from being murdered. I was unconscious at the time, so I have no memory of him being there, but I remember meeting him in the hospital that I woke up in 8 months after the incident occurred and felt then like I knew him. Let me tell you the whole story.

Right now, it is some 6 years from the time I was a victim of murder, so not everything is going to be in here. I will put in what I remember.

George was born in a toy shop in Southern California in November 2013. He immediately put himself into the business of putting himself for sale in the location near Krishna. Krishna... I shall call her Krishna from here on out... was a Veteran of the United States Marine Corps and a female of great strength and fortitude. She was a Nurse at the Veteran's Affairs (VA) Hospital in San Diego, California. I had met her there, and she was living with me. I am also a Veteran of the USMC, who served as a sniper and a Force Reconnaissance Marine for 11 years. In November 2013 I was out of the military for 9 years and had been in Phoenix, Arizona near the VA Hospital there and they kicked me out and left me to get hit by a truck, which broke both my legs, my knee, my foot, my back, my face, my nose, and my skull. Horrible. I was put in the Hospital there and was in a coma for two months, and unconscious for 8 months straight.

And George arrived during that time and saved my life. Krishna brought him. She spoke for him, a lot of lifesaving and pleasant things to me. I remember that was in my mind when she brought him to the VA Medical Center in Loma Linda, California, where I was being treated for the ability to walk and surgery on my knee. I regained consciousness there in July 2014. George showed up in August 2014 and I was so happy to see him! I didn't remember him, but there was something in my mind that drew me to him... from experience with him. I can't explain it. Well, actually, I just did! That was what had happened. My brain cells were dying and being replaced by brain cells that were nearby, so I didn't have an accurate memory of what had happened, but I had a parallel to it that mattered a lot! That is how brain damage happens!

George speaks to me through Krishna. I have the premonition that he is actually speaking to me through her as a means to communicate to me readily. It is through the onset of the magic capabilities of the forces in the atmosphere that he is able to put his ideas through space and time to Krishna's head and to put in there the ideas of speech that she finds pervading her. That is how it works, on a magical note of power. Thus, his ideas are actual and real and coming from the lion's head, even if it is coming out of Krishna's mouth. I am going to start out writing about things he has said to me by saying it as "Krishna said in George's voice...(whatever)". But then as time continues, I will begin to explain it as it truly is... "George said...(whatever)." That will put it in the terms that reflect reality.

How can a person have such a thing as an "Active Doll" in his mind in a way that doesn't spell "insanity"? Read on and you will see how it is interpreted. The person who is having these images is highly intelligent. I have an IQ of 142 or higher, and it is probably the same even with the onset of brain damage. Thus, some of the things I explain may not make any sense to you... like the onset of the actions of a Lion Doll... but they are real and seen by someone with a higher intelligence than all but 1% of the population. So, there, you! Read on and get it through your head that your Dolls may be actually trying to communicate with you!

Now, onto some more about George's past.

First off, let me let you know that I am writing another book right now that is titled: *Death and Life as a Victim of Vehicular Homicide.* It has nothing in it about George. I used to think that he was a Doll and people would think I was crazy if I talked about him like he had human characteristics. But now I don't care. I shall write a book about him and see how it turns out.

The first place that I remember coming into contact with George, and remember that my memory was gone for 8 months so there are parts that I have no memory of, the first place I have a memory of George being there was inside of the Loma Linda VA Hospital in Southern California. I was being taught how to walk again after having my legs broken. I was laying in my bed in D Unit and Krishna came in with George in her hands and brought me some food. She told me that George was there to help me eat it. I didn't remember him, but he seemed very familiar. I told her so.

She lay the food out of the bag and in her voice, George started to tell me what food tasted good and what food was questionable. "Eat the WheatChex... it is good for you! How do your legs feel? Hard walking on them, isn't it? Think about kicking them outwards, that should do the trick! What, am I saying things that are obtrusive? Whatever do you mean? Get over it! I am a Lion and I say things the way that they are! So, get over it!" He was a really intelligent lion, but men, was he saying things that were a pain in the ass! But that is what a patient gets when they are in the hospital with a caregiver that knows the details about the sickness that is pervading the body of the wounded.

Today is September 1st, 2019 and I told Krishna that I was writing a book about George. She asked how it went, and I told her that I had to ask her some background questions about him being at the hospitals where I was unconscious. She told me that he wasn't at any of those... that she got him when I was at the Loma Linda VA Hospital. So, my earlier recollection of him being present was wrong. But he still seemed very familiar to me. Perhaps it was his fluctuating beams of energy transmitting through space when he was made to me because he and I were to become soulmates. Perhaps!

I am going to ask Krishna and George more questions about our relationship this afternoon, or tomorrow when she isn't working, I think. I shall ask her questions like: "Where did you get him?" "What was buying him like?" "How did you pick him out?" "What ideas did he give to you?" And questions like that will be asked. The answers will be interesting, I think!

I told Krishna: "I am writing a book about George and I wonder... what does he think about that?"

George responded in his voice and Krishna's lyrics: "I am an excellent lion! I like you a lot, papas, I really do! What are you going to write about me? What? Is it fun? What does it say? What?" And he took a break, then he said: "You don't think I'm rude, do you? I know you don't!" That was George for you... correcting himself as he spoke.

I told him: "You are absolutely correct! You are an outstanding lion, you are! And the rest was correct, too! Good job!"

He chuckled. He likes the plethora of good comments.

Then Krishna went back to sleep. I had to wait until later to get back in touch with George.


Today I asked Krishna: "Where did you pick up George when you got him for me? Do you remember?"

"I don't remember," she said. "Was it in Barbados? I was on a trip to Barbados around that time..."

"Around the time that you brought him to the Hospital in Loma Linda?"

"Yea, around then. I don't remember getting him. Strange. It was a long time ago."

"It was about 6 years and a few months ago." I was clear on that.

"Oh, it was. I didn't think of that. Strange." She changed the subject.

Later I asked her other questions. We were driving with my Service Dog to the VA Hospital to pick up some medicines.

I asked Krishna what George said to her after she had gotten him but before they came to Loma Linda to see me for the first time. Krishna told me, in George's voice: "Oh wow! We are going to meet a Marine? A friend of yours? That is stupendously fantastic! He is a Veteran, you say? That is magnificent! I shall keep it in my Highest Honor to give him a lot of service! That will be my Pride and Joy..." He was so happy!

Then Krishna brought him to the VA Hospital to see and visit with me for the first time. "I am so happy to see you, papa! I am going to call you that forevermore... papa. That is your name... papa Krautant! I've got it! You would be astonished by what I know..." that was what George said to me... "I know about secrets of all matter and how light moves in space and how people have Souls and what those Souls can do!" That was remarkable, and I believed him. I still do.

As we were sitting on the bed in D Unit of the VA Hospital in Loma Linda Krishna broke out some food from a box she had brought... a LOT of food... mostly snacks and milk-to-be-laden cereal bars and such food. The food she explained to me was extremely healthy, and George replied to her comments: "Yes, this food is really good for you. Take my word on it. It is healthy for a man in such bad condition like you are in. Man, you are so skinny! You need to eat your snacks and cereal! Put some milk on there you heroic natured beast! The fibers in the lentils will do you some good, as will the fibers in the jerky! That is made of beef, see! A real animal with the hooves of plentitude! See what I mean?" He was having a really funny and interesting conversation with me. I didn't know what to say.

I said: "Yeah, yeah, I see what you mean. You are a funny lion! What do you say to the cereal?"

George said: "Wheat Chex, which you are eating, has no artificial color, no artificial flavor, and is made from Whole Wheat that is definitely good for your bone and muscles. That is what you are eating! The cereal is good for you, possibly one of the best sources of protein there is in the morning for you! Interesting, isn't it?" He said it in a cheery and happy voice, with an instructive tone. He sounded like a professor from a college for Kids speaking to his student body. And they liked him a lot! That is how I felt, and he could sense it in his stationary, silly Lion's body laying flat on my bed with his arms stamped outwards and his legs splayed out. I had put him on my bed so I could hear him speak to me. Granted, he spoke to me in pleasant tones in the voice of Krishna... but it wasn't her voice speaking. It was George's. I could tell that from the beginning. I even began to look at him on the bed when he was speaking to me so I could see his body move. It didn't, but my imagination went to work and made it move imaginary.

I know that because at the time I was recovering from brain damage and had some strange things happening with my mind. George was a pleasant addition to that. A real Doll with real humanitarian actions to help me... me a damaged partner.

We spent the day getting medicine at the VA Hospital in Loma Linda, then went home. Krishna went to sleep because she had to work that night, so the conversation ended.

What else did George say about my care inside of the Loma Linda VA Hospital? I am going to ask Krishna and George and see what they remember.

We were driving down from Krishna's cabin in the mountains to our home in town, about 2 hours away, and George was asked the following question: "Hey George, I know you like sitting on the console in the front of the car, so tell me, what did we talk about at the Loma Linda VA Hospital in 2014 when you came to visit me there for the first time?" I was calm in asking him.

"You are a resolute hero, a legend! And I shall call you "Pops" or "Papa", right? Which do you prefer?" He was well spoken and loud in his comments. I could tell he really felt them stably.

"Well, Krishna calls her brother "Pops" so that won't do. Call me "Papa Krautant", won't you?"

"Ok, ok, ok! I think you are an excellent hero, papa

Krautant! I have a full rendition of what you did in the military from our minds. Didn't know I could "read your mind", did you? I can, I can! That is what happens when a person who is almost killed comes into contact with a Lion who wants to save them! And I will, I will! I shall give you the best care you could even imagine! Believe that!" George was really well-spoken.

I responded about the subject he just talked about. "That is good, George. Was I an aspect of your Creation… the way that God was a part of our Creation? Not that I am God or anything, but just a part in your Creation."

"Well, if you put it like that, then yes, you WERE you WERE a part of my Creation! The elements of my mind and the put together of my mentality are parts of your brain coming in line with my brain and making the thoughts arise! It is interesting! You would call it "Physics" … and that is what it is, too! Physics! And secret nature, too! A secret! Because there is no way to mathematically put together a theory that equals the transmission of thought from a Lion to a person anyways. Try it, and you will fail! You will come up with some headlong theory that makes no sense that is made up of fiction and circumstances… not reality! That is what you will get!" George was speaking really elegantly, thus the name of this story!

I responded. "So, I was a part of your Creation. That is remarkable! How do you feel about it?"

"I feel outstanding! It is a good sense of being to me a part of a special person's life. And now you are a Service Dog handler, too! I was expecting such a thing from you after the incident. I don't remember the years... I am horrible with years... but it was recently, right? You did a good job at it, passing the class and everything. I remember you coming into the house when you were getting ready to have her and you were in the class to get her... you were studying and studying and studying and telling the Commands out loud and everything to get ready to earn her. And you DID, you DID!"

Then there was a pause in the conversation as I looked back at my Service Dog Paige in the back seat and said "hi" to her. Then George began to speak again.

"Hey, papa, I heard from Krishna that you two had walked in the snow from your cabin in the mountains towards town around the curves and down a narrow road about 12 miles! Man, that is a longways to go! Do you think you could do it again?" George was excited!

"No, George, I wouldn't be able to do it again. My leg was broken during the incident with the truck in 2013 and you saw me recovering in 2014, but my leg was still injured, and it still is injured. It hurts when I walk on it. So, no, no walking 12 miles in the snow for me anymore... And as far as dates go, it was 2015 that I put in for a grant to get a Service Dog through the Canine Support Teams, and they raised a Dog for 2 years until 2017 for me, and in 2017 I went to a course to get her, and I passed it!"

"I can't remember those dates, papa. What are you telling them to me for? Whoa! Look at those cars passing us! They are going to collide with us!" George was waving his head around looking out the window.

"Are you talking about those cars moving behind us?"

"Yeah, papa, the speed limit here is 25 miles per hour and those fools are speeding up to 45 miles per hour trying to pass us! Stupid fools! They are going to cause a wreck!" George was really upset over those idiot cars. They had no concept of the fact that they were in the realm of creating a wreck with their errant driving. It was horrible to have to drive in that kind of traffic... and it was everywhere! There was car after car speeding by us, and Krishna drives at the speed limit everywhere she goes. So, it seems like it is only a matter of time before she gets into a collision with some errant car driving recklessly. There are a lot of them out there!

George put the conversation on Pause for a while as we drove on the freeway. Me and Krishna finally got hungry and went to the Chicken Shop to get some deep-fried chicken to eat. We went through the drive through, and George looked at the advertisement sign on the window of the building and said: "Look, guys! That is a Fierce Lion like me! Raargh! I want some! I want some! And I don't even know what they are!"

It was a picture of Honeyed Chicken on a Bun, a dessert that nobody on a diet in our car would get. That is, except George! Well, my Service Dog probably would, too, but she wasn't picking then. We laughed and got our chicken. I gave some to George to sample. He liked it! I gave him some more then he said he had a full stomach.

We drove for a little while more and got home. George was asleep. Krishna brought him into the house and put him on my bed to stay asleep.

I put my new CONTINUOUS POSITIVE AIRWAY PRESSURE (CPAP) machine together and got ready to use it. I have severe sleep apnea and will probably die if I don't use something to control my breathing while I sleep. George replied to my request for a comment when we had just gotten the CPAP machine from the VA Hospital with a nice meeting with the technician. We got back in the car where George was waiting for us and he said: "It is so nice that you have a CPAPA machine now, papa! That's right... I called it a CPAPa machine! That is because it was made for you and your care! You shall do excellent at it... I am sure of that! Can I help? Just let me know what I need to say to be of assistance!"

What George didn't realize back at the house when he was asleep was that I connected myself to the CPAP and started to breath out of it. I had read the instruction manual before I did it and the instructions said that the TV shouldn't be on and there should be no listening to the radio when one is on the CPAP machine. So, while I usually listened to the TV radio station when I went to sleep, I turned it off and put in the CPAP. I didn't sleep for 2 hours. So, not sleeping, I put on the TV on the music channel and listened to the radio and fell asleep. The apnea kicked on when I did it, and when I woke up, I was tired and felt like I didn't rest. It was probably me not being used to the breathing apparatus being on me that did it.

My sleep schedule on the CPAP said that I was asleep for 5 ½ hours. I only remember being asleep for 2. But I was connected to it for 5 ½... from 10:30 to 4 – something. That shows that I have a severe sleep apnea that it is going to take time and treatment to recover from.

George stayed asleep throughout the entire episode. I am going to go ask Krishna what came of his thoughts to the CPAP and why I didn't feel rested afterwards and didn't sleep during the time it was on. We'll see what he has to say about it.

I asked Krishna this afternoon what George thought about the fact that I had only gotten 2 hours of sleep that night with the CPAP machine on, and she said that she had checked on me and I had gotten a lot more than 2 hours of sleep. But I felt tired when I woke up at 4 in the morning, and she didn't say anything about that. She said that her patients at the VA hospital who had CPAP machines would watch TV and listen to the TV radio when they were using the CPAP, so I should as well. So, that is what I am going to do from here on out. I shall put the TV radio on like I used to in order to go to sleep.

I will talk to George on my own and take his answers out of my own mind and put them within this story about him. He gives me ideas that are positive about things, and hopefully he will be able to help me get some sleep that is positive with the CPAP machine.

Later, Krishna was getting ready to go to work and was leaving out the front door. I was standing there to shut the garage door. I said to her: "Tell George that I will be writing about him tonight."

"You'll be writing about me, papa? That is so nice of you! What will you write in your story? Will it be good? I hope it is good stuff!" George was cheery.

"I shall be interviewing you while Thumbs is gone so I can get your answers within my own mind. Stuff about science! I am going to interview you about physics and quality things like that!" I said it firmly and nicely.

"I know science like nobody's business, papa! I know ALL THE THINGS THERE ARE TO KNOW ABOUT SCIENCE! I can answer your questions, yes I can! Yes I can!" George was ebullient!

"I've got to go, Krautant. Take it easy, George! I love you, you Lion!" Krishna was pleased with our conversation.

"I am a remarkable Lion! Raargh! That is like what you say in the military, isn't it?"

"We say "Oooh Rah in the Marines…"

"Well, Raaa Raaah is what I am going to say in the world of the Steadfast Lion! Raaa Raaah!"

"Ok, George. See ya, Krishna." She walked out the garage door and I closed it and locked it behind her.

Then I came back to the room and began to write.

"Papa, I know what you should write... do some recon on how to make Gulab Jaan! That is what you should do!" George was excitable.

"How do you spell Gulab Jaan, George?" I asked him because I didn't really know how to spell it.

"G-U-L-A-B J-A-A-N...that is how you spell it!" George was really smart... I could tell!

Then Peter the Rabbit spoke from his fiber metal jar with my medicines in it on the counter: "Hey papa, I see you are getting some tea made. What does tea taste like? I've never had any..." Peter spoke in kind and pleasant terms and terminology and had a peaceful voice about him. That was appropriate for a tiny little rabbit.

"Here Peter, you wanna try some?" I asked him. Krishna brought over the mug of tea and we swept his head into the mug so he could taste it. He slobbered a little and gasped.

"Oh papa, it is so sweet! I don't know if I like it! It is so cold!" Peter was gasping.

"IT'S ICED TEA, PETER! It is made on ice! That

is why it is so cold! I like it because it is delicious!" I was clear on that one.

"You're right papa, it IS delicious. Perhaps I DO like it. But I am not used to the cold. I will have to try it out again and see if I am used to it. Until then... ta da!" And with that Peter went back into his Lion and rested.

"Raaargh!" said George. "Will you make ME into a Recon Marine, papa? I have the skills and the ferocity! I shall be a fiestious lion, I will! Watch me prevail over the weak! I will destroy them all! Watch me!"

"I believe you George, I believe you!"

And with that the conversation continued, but I am writing this statement later, so I don't remember what exactly was said. But I do remember that I got eggs and toast and we talked about something totally unrelated to them. But I don't remember what. Oh well. I shall write about our conversations later

- Of note... there are a lot of people at the Coffee Shop reading books of information and solid reading. That is an indicator that people like to get ideas from other people in their writings. And it leads me to the conclusion that many of you readers of THIS book will really enjoy it and like what it says about GEORGE THE ELEGANT LION! Yes, indeeeeedy! And that goes for my other books as well... I am not going to list their names because by the time this book comes out there will probably be other books written... but I definitely hope you enjoy them! Check my name online and it will have a list of the books I have written!

"Hey papa, how do you think your health is doing? I think it is doing excellently! What do you say about the symbiosis of my statements? I recognize that is a big word. Perhaps it is too big for you to take on for actual meaning. Well, which is it, papa? Is it too big a word for you? I didn't think it was! That is my understanding of you... that you know a lot of words. Didn't know that I was made adept at understanding your intelligence, did you? Did you, papa? I just asked you a question and I want an answer! Did you know, by the ways that I speak to you? Did you know? Did you?" George was silent then after his long speech, waiting for an answer. Or... Answers to multiple questions!

I answered him one question at a time. "George, you speak to me really intelligently, and you wouldn't do so if you didn't think I was intelligent enough to understand you! And in-regards-to the term "symbiosis", all I have to do is look up the term online and get the definition of it. For example, the term "symbiosis" means: "interaction between two different organisms living in close physical association, typically to the advantage of both." That is the Wikipedia online definition of the word. So there, George... I have access to the knowledge of the tools to find the answers to the questions!" I was quiet then and let him answer with another question.

"That is so good of you, papa! That shows that you have the intelligence to bring your health to the forefront of your existence! It will come in good for you considering the fact that you had to settle for a really minor sum of money from the lawsuit you were involved in against the VA for their abuse of power and refusal to give you medicines and that ended in the bad result of you getting images and illusions and getting hit by a truck and nearly killed. Actually, you have a memory of dying in the coma in the hospital, don't you? That is not surprising, papa. It was horrible what happened to you. And it is pitiful that the VA isn't paying their veteran a decent amount so he can get care for his disabilities that are still present. Horrible. What else can I say about it? It is Horrible, papa! Horrible!" George was really going off with his speech. He had a lot to say, and he was really talkative tonight.

"George, you know better than any other that I spend a lot of time thinking about my health... both mental and physical. That is in part because I can't drive anywhere, so if something negative happens to me and my health goes bad I will have to wait for Krishna to come home from work to take me to the doctor's office in Loma Linda. That is a whole hour away, too. And she'll want to sleep. Sometimes she comes home tired and ready for bed and doesn't walk the dogs because she is too tired. So, even if I am sick, she might not be able to drive me to Loma Linda VA Hospital safely. I don't know. I am only guessing." I wanted to be clear with my points. And I was. George answered that he understood what I was talking about, and he was sure that Krishna had what it took in her to make ways for the trip as needed from her, regardless if she had been working or not.

I thanked George for the excellent input. Then George asked me if I enjoyed the movie that I saw tonight.

"The movie was excellent. It was really good acting by Brad Pitt. He is a good actor anyways, but he went far above and beyond in his acting in this movie. I really liked it. It went into astronauts in such detail that it seemed very realistic. It didn't even seem like Hwood film... it seemed like a real video footage of actual events in the Real World. Interesting!" I really enjoyed the movie. I am leaving the title out of this story because I don't want to have to get permissions to advertise it. But it was an excellent movie!

"That is good to hear, papa. Good to hear! Watch some of your Cooking Channel now. I shall be quiet. I have talked enough for tonight." George was through talking and was quiet after that statement.

"Ok, George. This show is about bad chefs. Interesting! I shall talk to you later, you fantastic Lion!"

"Thank you papa! Good night!"

"Good night, George."


George spoke up a lot today. He asked me: "Hey papa, what do you think about the legs of a lion? I am a

Ferocious Lion... with personality! What do you think about my legs?"

"What about your legs? Can you do special things with your legs?" I asked him.

"I can wave my legs side-to-side without bending them, in conflict with Gravity! I can deny Gravity the flow and presence of being! That is what I can do... and I do it on a regular basis! Want me to show you?" George was all excited. He liked his superpowers the way a superhero would enjoy being a superhero.

"George, you can't show me right now because you are in the house and we are in the car!" I said it absolutely.

"Oh papa, that is too bad. I really wanted to show you the miracle! Can I show you when you get home?" He was still explanatory: "Actually, I can show you now! Didn't know I could flow through space and time in your mind to your imagination while you are 3-miles down the street in the car and I am locked in the house, did you? Imagine me standing in front of you... can you see me? Now, imagine my legs flowing upwards over my head... can you see it? Good! That is using your imagination to envision that which you should not be able to see! It is MAGIC... see? YOU DO, YOU DO! I can see you, too! Nice, isn't it?" George was so happy being able to stand for our imagination from a far-away distance. He was very pleased with himself. And he was able to see us, too, from his distance away, which was part of the miracle. He was a Lion of Miracles, he was!

Then I asked him about the conversation I had with Krishna about the phone call she got from the author I was trying to get to edit my *Cheetah on the Wing* books. She said: "The author couldn't get through to the publisher yet. She is working on it. She expects to get ahold of him today. She plans on calling us tomorrow between 8 and 8:30. Sorry! Hope you get published..."

George responded: "That was so nice of her! I hope you get published too! That is an interesting story! I was around when you were writing it. You had a fantastic thoroughfare with the computer that you were writing on. How many different ways did you try to write the story? A dozen or so? You were overcoming brain damage when you were writing it, weren't you? I know you were! You did a remarkable job with writing it. I know that you have an IQ of 142, though... is that too much to write so that people can understand it? I hope not. Hopefully that author will get you manuscript edited so that she can tell you what needs to be written in a simpler manner for all readers to understand."

That was all of the conversation I had with George at that time. He was really appreciative of my writing abilities. I appreciated it! I even said: "Thank you for your insight!" to him. He just smiled.

"Man!" said George, gasping... "Man you stink!"

"Whatever do you mean, George?" I asked him.

"Not you, papa... ma! Krishna stinks like high

Heaven! It's her farts! She's stinking up the whole house! My God! Eeeew!" George was panting out loud. "Do something about it, papa!"

"George, you KNOW that I can't smell! I can't even tell that she is farting! I can't hear it, either!" I didn't believe him. But I had to listen to him talk about it, because it *was* true that I couldn't smell, so there *was a chance* that she did in fact fart, and I didn't sense it.

"I don't care if you can smell or not! I am saying it and I'll say it again: SHE FARTED! And it STANK! It is that nasty beef that she ate from the Mexican Restaurant today. You went there with her, so you should know. And it is making her FART!" He said it in a totally rambunctious tone, like he wanted to discipline me for not being able to smell the farts.

I was getting out of control at George's tones: "Get over it George! It doesn't make that big of a deal! What if *you* begin to fart? You're a Lion that eats meat... so what is there to stop *you* from farting? What? Answer me!" I was getting tense in my tone.

"Nothing, papa... nothing. I am sorry. I didn't mean to upset you. I just wish you could smell... that is all."

"Well, I can't. My nose got broken during the vehicular homicide I was a victim of. And those VA idiots are paying me very little for it. What do you think about THAT?"

"They are horrible idiots, papa! I wish they would go to Hell for what they did to you!"

"So do I, George. So do I."

And that ended that conversation.

George was speaking indebtedly tonight, at first. "Papa. What are we going to do in China? What is the means of our transportation there? I mean, we are going to the Great Wall of China, right? What are we going to do there? You can't walk all the way up there because your leg is damaged, right? So, what are you going to do there? What?"

I didn't know how to answer him. There was nothing I could do. "I am not going to do anything. I am just going to walk up the stairs a little, then I am going to come back down and wait for Krishna to come down." I couldn't think of any other way it would go.

"Ok, papa; I can accept that. So long as nothing bad happens to Krishna and she isn't able to come down to see you again. What if she has a heart attack there?" George was using a loud voice for that question, and it was obstructing Krishna's well-being.

"It won't happen, George! Stop saying that! You're going to put me in a heart attack now if you don't shut up!" Krishna was upset over the topic even being mentioned.

"Ok, Krishna, Ok! Sorry!" George was apologizing profusely. "Let me change the subject, like I always do. Papa, I am so glad you are working on getting published. You deserve it! I want to read your first book. Can I can

I can I? Huh? Can I? What do you say to that? Get me your first book!"

"George, the first book is going to go to a buyer of the books. I don't want to keep it from them. I have copies of the books already printed out on my desk in a file cabinet. You can read that. I will get it ready for you, okay?" I was not really sure what his answer would be to that. Probably a negative... and that is what it was.

"Papa, I have money to buy the book! A lot of money saved up! I have enough I think, too!"

"George, it is going to cost some $12. You don't have that..."

"Papa, I have $11 and 99 cents. That is enough, isn't it? I can get the veteran's groups to help pay for it if it isn't enough, right? Right, I say?" George was confident that he could get the book.

"Ok, George, ok... you can do it. And if you disrupt the book in any way or form, you can read my printed copy of the book, too. Ok?" I was trying to please George.

"Ok, papa, Ok. Another question..." George was curious tonight.

"What is that, George? Is it about why the VA is so corrupt and didn't give me hardly any money for my settlement?" I thought that was what he was going to ask me.

"Yeah, papa, yeah. Those idiots at the VA Hospital deserve to be punished for what they did to you. Same for the prison people. They all deserve nothing less than Hell! HELL! That is what they deserve!" George was yelling. "They deserve to burn in the deepest fires of the pits of Hell for their malfeasances! They deserve PAIN and MISERY! They deserve to fall deep!"

I answered readily: "Yep, George, Hell is what they deserve, and Hell is what they will get! God has already agreed that they are going to go to Hell, and that is what they deserve!" I was yelling too.

"Papa, God has told me at my request that I am going to be allowed to go to Hell to stand at the gates of it and to set those idiots on fire there and to watch them burn with the deepest FIRES of HELL! He said I deserve that justice! He said YOU deserve that justice too!" George was well-spoken.

I was also well-spoken: "George, that is wonderful to hear that God would do such an honorable and Holy thing for you! He has agreed to let you sit at the gates of Hell and to set those villains on fire? That is what they deserve! How honorable of you to accept such honors!" I was very pleased with George. And it was a miracle that he could tell me such things about Hell in Krishna's voice (because he was a Lion in a doll's body, so he wasn't supposed to speak. But he was under the auspices of miracle workerhood, and it processed the changes through light and thought to process the speech of a Lion through the body of a nurse.)

"That is how it is, papa! God is an Honorable Hero! He

wants the best for all of us. And the things those people did against you were illegal and deserve to be punished as a whole! And they will! Have Faith! They WILL!"

"I believe you George! I believe you!"

The conversation proceeded onto talking about writing. But he talked about what to write here about him. But I forgot what he said about it. I think I have already written it down here. We'll see what I write later. I'll ask him about what we talked about so I can put it down here.

Until then... see ya!


Today, Peter the Rabbit spoke to me. It was followed by Pete the Lion saying things. Then I got spoken to by George. He said: "You think that was terrible the nightmare that Peter Rabbit had about MacGor killing his sister? Let me tell you what I am going to do to that beast for even coming up in a nightmare and doing such a horrible thing! I am going to take out my rifle and pummel him to death! Beaten to a pulp... that is what is going to happen to him! And he is going to moan and wail in agony as I pulverize his ass into a tiny little wimp of a man! That is what is going to happen to him! There will be no recompense for his utter tears spilling from his eyes and cheeks! He shall suffer, and we shall enjoy it! Yes! That is what is going to be done about him!" George was ebullient about his message.

"Those are some good points George," I said to him. "Are you going to put those skills to work when I

teach you about how to go to war? It is written about
in a future chapter. Would you like to peruse it?" I was
thinking about moving through the story about *George the
Elegant Lion* and writing about different parts at different
times... but in such a manner that the content wouldn't
be repeated unnecessarily in further put chapters. We'll
see how it works out.

"Sure, papa. Take me to the chapter titled *Me and
George the Lion go to War.*"

So, I did. Transfer to that chapter and you will see
how we spoke about war. You'll like it or be disturbed by
it. Either way... you will appreciate it!

"Papa papa! I have a name for me! Can you change it,
can you? My last name should be MARSOC! That would
be an elegant name for me! It fits into my Lion's warfare
capabilities! How does that sound to YOU, papa? How
does it sound? It sounds miraculous to me!" George was
really eager to get me to change his name to MARSOC.
I wondered if he knew what it meant.

"Do you know what MARSOC stands for, George?
It stands for Marine Amphibious Reconnaissance Special
Operations Capable unit. That is what I used to belong to.
And like they say... Once a Marine, Always a Marine!"
I was trying to speak very calmly to him, because I knew
that he was going to add some more to his rudimentary
speech. Then again, perhaps it wasn't "rudimentary" ...
because it had to do with Special Forces.

"Papa, that is definitely what my name should be! I want to go to war with you, too! That name takes up all the hallmarks of well-being among the forces of Good in the Universe! And there is more to it than that..." George was ebullient and carrying on with gusto.

"What is that, George?" I asked.

"YOU should change your last name to MARSOC, too! You could change the name of your author to Mitchell MARSOC! That would be a solid name!" George was not ready for another answer.

But he got one. "My name on my books is Mitchell Krautant. That is my name, George, so I don't want to change it to something else!" I was adamant about that answer.

"What do you think that George the Rabbit thinks about that? I bet you that he doesn't like it! What do you say, Peter?" George was really carrying on now.

"Whimper whimper, whimper!" said Peter Rabbit. "I don't like it... but whatever papa wants to do is up to him to do!"

"That is not supposed to be your answer!" shouted George.

"Whimper whimper... okay George... okay! But I mean what I said!" Peter was real firmly spoken in his meanings and wanted us to see his side of things.

George responded with a question: "What do you think Pete says about it? Hmm? What do YOU say, Pete?"

I responded with another question to clarify what he meant... "You said the term "Pete". Do you mean Peter the Rabbit or Pete the Lion? Which do you mean?"

Pete the Lion spoke up: "He meant Pete the Lion! And I think that papa is right in saying that he is sticking with his given name. It would be too much for him to name himself "MARSOC" because the people who looked up that name online would say negative things about him for using it. So no, he SHOULDN'T use it!"

"That says that!" said Peter Rabbit, yelling loudly! "That takes my side of things! That makes me want to ROAR! ROAR!"

"ROAR!" shouted Pete the Lion! And he laughed out loud!

George stayed silent and didn't say anything, his beard waggling, in creases, throughout his face.

Then we arrived at the coffee shop. I went in for some coffee. George and the Peters stayed in the house and said nothing.

George spoke up to me when I came home: "Hey papa, what would you say if I learned how to type and edited your book about me? What would you say to that? Would it make you happy?"

"What would you say?" I asked George.

"I would say all kinds of nice and remarkable things about how you spend time writing even in the dark and you think a lot about it and tell the story in lyrics and words that are steady in production and that make a lot of sense in a higher ramifications of existence. That is what I would say... and it is accurate!" George was trying to speak calmly to me.

I responded in kind: "George, that would be so nice of you. I could put you on a blog on my book website. What do you say about that?" I was serious about that, too.

"That would be excellent papa! I would speak really well about your books. I have to read them though, first. The people who read over your books should be able to read over them in China, too, I think. They would be able to read and understand your books, too, because all they have to do is move their fingers over the words and take on the syllables within their mental process for communication. That would fix that problem!" George was well-spoken, even though he was changing the subject matter of the conversation.

"That would do the trick, George. How did you know about such a thing about another culture?"

"Because I have the capability to envision differences between cultures like reading different syllables in words that look similar to each other but have different letters in them. The sound of the verbs and nouns is what matters the most in such a distinction and interpretation! That is what matters the most! Understand?" George was moving his hand side-to-side to get the structure of his sentences out wholesale so I could understand them. Not that it was necessary... because what he said made sense in my mind.

"Ok, George, I understand what you mean. I am going to go and sit down and begin to write down what I can remember about the lengthy conversations we just had about things. My memory is already vacant on a lot of it, but I will try to write down what I can remember and make up the rest. What do you say??" I was solid about that process.

"That sounds good to me, papa. Let me know what to do with your mind and I will transcribe the images of the being of the Lion to you to write about in your book about me!"

"That will be good, George. I will let you know when I am aware of it. I shall think about it tonight."

"Thank you papa! Thank you!"

And with that, the conversation was over... for now.


George began to carry on today about things that meant nothing to anyone but me: "Papa! Papa! Let me tell you something! You are a Lion like me, and that is coming from a Lion of an aggressive nature! You are a Hero! A rendition of Hercules! That is right, papa! You are a legend in your own making! How were you created? Out of the thoroughfare of legendary status! That is what you are made out of! I should know because I was designed in your image... and look at me! LOOK AT ME! I am a FEROCIOUS LION! That is what I am, and that is what you are too, papa! What do you think about that?" George was panting aloud, and he liked it! He raised his hackles up in the air and patted them around him readily. He wanted to strike the enemy and bring them to retribution!

"That is the way to go about describing me, George! Thank you for that!" I was pleased with him. Then I asked him: "What to the Peters say about that? Can you tell me?"

George responded quickly: "They like it papa! They like it a lot! They can't say anything to you right now because they are talking about your greetings by me. And they like it *a lot!* And that is what you think about the thoroughfare I gave you, isn't it? That you like it, papa?" George was curious, but he should have known the answer. After all, he was a part of me, so he should have known what was going through my mind. There was a space between the thoughts I had and him, though. I could tell by the errant ways he talked sometimes. But most of the time his intelligence came out.

I wondered if his intelligence reflected MY intelligence. I wondered...

So, I asked him: "Hey George, this is a sidebar question... I am wondering if I can ask you it?"

"Go ahead, papa..."

"I am wondering if your intelligence reflects my intelligence. After all, you were CREATED after me...

so that makes your intelligence a reflection of mine, right?" I was hoping I got that statement accurately.

"Well, that may be the case... but then again... it could be that YOUR intelligence is a reflection of MINE... get it?" George was standing with his hands on his hips in a semblance of authority and it made him in a position of completeness. He seemed to know what he was talking about, even though it flew in the face of common sense. Perhaps it was so... it just took a Lion Doll to understand how that could be!

"Ok, George, I believe you may be right. How many pages have I written in this section about what the Lion George did for the Veteran? About 29?" I was counting pages. What was wrong with me?

"It is 30 pages. Are you going to write more about it?" George was wondering.

"I am going to write some in the next chapter. I will get Krishna to talk about Peter the Rabbit and Pete the Lion. That will bring about enough to write about on those subjects, I think!" I was hoping I was clear.

"I think you should save some room to write some more in this chapter" said George. He was absolutely positive on that reflection.

"Ok. I will. Are we done talking for now?" I asked him.

"That is all for now, papa. You are a Hercules! A Superman!"

"Thank you George. Is that all?"

"That is all, papa. Have a nice night."

"You too, George. You too!"


"George, I am heading out of the kitchen and into my room. Do you want to come with me?" I asked George nicely.

"Yeah, papa! I have had a remarkable time with Peter the Rabbit sitting here and eating your chicken. He didn't have any because he is a Vegetarian, you know, but I had some chicken breast and it was deeeeelicious! I would like some more as time progresses. Can I have some later? Can I can I can I? What do you say, papa? Can I?" George was excitable and carrying on a lot!

I was patient with him. "Sure, you can have some chicken later. Now, do you want to come and write with me?"

"Yes papa, I would like to write with you a LOT! I can look at the computer, can't I? I can write out sentences and big words and phrases that mean things that you wouldn't ordinarily think of them being able to mean... and it would be excellent! EXCELLENT! What do you say to me taking part in the writing? What do you say? Huh? What is that?" George was extremely curious about writing and really wanted to join me with it.

I asked him a question in that regards: "George, do you think that you can transcribe into my mind the thoughts of writing words and letters and sentences in such a bright manner that it will give me the ideas you have to help me write them out?"

"I certainly can, papa! *I CAN!* That is my skills as a Lion... to put forth my thoughts and ideas forthwith! I can do it and I will! So, take me to your room and let me lay next to you and look at your computer and see what is being typed!" George was excited to do it.

"Ok, George, come on!" I took him into the room and placed him on the bed next to my pillow and lay back against the pillow and got on the computer. "See George," I said to him, "I am writing this out now from the memories that I am getting from you! So, the question is this... did you tell me to write a sentence about writing memories from you... or did I come up with that memory myself?" I was wondering.

"I'll never tell!" said George. He was smiling. And he was pleased with himself. He must have really liked what I had written.

And that was it for tonight... or at least this chapter. The rest of the book shall be done later.

That is all. And that is how the Lion named George rescued a Veteran of Force Reconnaissance Company! Very nice!

Read on!

# CHAPTER 2

## THE COMBINATION OF GEORGE WITH PEARLE, PEACHES, PETER THE LION AND PETER THE RABBIT

Soon after having George come into my company, me and Krishna and George went up to Seattle Washington and went around up there getting ready to get on a ship for a cruise to Alaska. There, we went in a car to a small town outside of Seattle that had a bunch of tiny stores in it. We went into one of the stores, and I had George in my backpack on my back, and I began to look at the dolls. George suddenly yelled: "Get that one! Get that one!" and in my hands was a doll of a small white unicorn that had dented feet. I liked it.

So, I got it.

It was remarkable that the status of the doll could be so remarkable. I immediately thought about the name I was going to call it. It was a female, and Krishna asked me what her name was going to be. So, I came up with a name after a little random thought and thought I would name her "Perle". I said it out-loud.

And Perle came back and said to me "That IS my name, you know, you strange hero!" Of course, she said it in Krishna's voice, but the nature and tone of the voice was not Krishna's... it belonged to Perle.

And that was the way we did it from there on out. The onset of Perle's voice was done through Krishna in the magical way that the doll does it. And it worked!

We departed the store and I brought Perle with me everywhere I went, for the most part. Granted, there was times when I wanted to walk along on the ship by myself and those times, I didn't take her with me. And sometimes it was annoying to have to hold onto her when I was sitting down, so I would leave her in the room. But all other times I brought her with me somewhere.

Perle turned out to be a really respectful unicorn. She pleases me with good comments about my well-being and positive things to do for the environment... namely things to talk about. She likes George. She also likes the other dolls I got after she came into contact.

One of them is a medium sized unicorn that is white that is named Peaches. Then, later, I got another lion doll named Peter. He is a small lion with fur on his head. Then finally I got Peter the Rabbit, who is wearing a green jacket just like the one in the cartoon movie about him. He is a small, steady Rabbit that is brown.

All of those creatures get along together really well, although sometimes George says some negative things about Peaches and Perle. He doesn't like that they are so pleasant and not aggravated. That's George for you. He is a rude animal sometimes, and talks back to me, the guy he saved from being near death. So, that is what is in his mind. That concludes for me. But he is a friend. That is the most important thing about him. And he saved my life!

Now let me talk about the characteristics of each Animal, so you can get a full symbiosis of what they are all about. I shall discuss them one-at-a-time, so you can get the full effect. But first, let me tell you about my mindset...

I had brain damage from the attempted homicide that I survived in 2013. It hadn't gone all the way's away as time progressed. I still had it in 2014 and 2015. It was 2014 that Krishna brought George into my room in the hospital to visit with me the first time. I liked him immediately. That was, in some ways, brain damage talking. But I responded to him speaking to me in Krishna's voice. And I have an IQ of 142... which is that of a Genius. Thus, I was able to put together in my own mind the ways and means that George was able to do things like move light around and do miraculous things with the mind and the being of people around him… thus, he was able to speak through Krishna in his own voice. It was the onset of physical energy throughout space and time from the onset of his mind to that of Krishna and her voice… and that made him unpredictable and special. He knew it, too! He told me so without Krishna being present!

Now, onto the conversation about the other animals…

Pearle and Peaches are very similar in the appearance of their demeanor. They are kind, intelligent, nice, pleasant beings. They have the capabilities of Unicorns… the magical powers imbued within themselves to do mystical things throughout the environment. They have been responsible, with George's help, in helping me be cured of the ailments that came from being broken all over the place. I have healed remarkably well, and I owe it to the mental proclivities of the Unicorns and the Lion to do such miraculous things for me. And it wasn't just those three that did it… Peter the Lion and Peter the Rabbit also helped to heal me. It may seem like a miracle, and it is! The mentality of the animals could have such a great effect on me that it is remarkable that it occurs.

"What do you want to do with your health?" said Perle through Krishna one day. I told her that I just wanted to be healthy. "Then think about the good things," she said through Krishna. I agreed and told her so. She smiled and said she was pleased. That is her character. She is pleased when I do a Good Thing for someone, and that includes offering quality comments.

Peaches usually offers comments after Perle is done talking. Her comments are usually about how some things are beyond her capability of doing them, and she only wants me to know about it. So, she explains in plain and simple terms. She knows that I have a really high intelligence, but that also I had brain damage, so she puts things in a simplistic manner so that I will definitely understand what the statements are all about. I do, too. I respond to her in kind... simplistic and easy to understand. That is good for speaking to Unicorns, because they are designed to explain things to the habitually stupid people too in a way that they can understand. That is what getting used to speaking to Unicorns is all about... getting used to speaking simply and plainly, even if you are high in intelligence.

I keep George the Lion and Peter the Lion and Perle and Peaches by the edge of the bed in my room. I talk to them sometimes, without Krishna being around to respond to me in their presence. I still get answers from them, in my mind. That is them using the forces of nature to portray a thought to me through space and time. Sounds bizarre, but when you start to talk to your animals and dolls, you will see that it has a true effect on the mind and memory. The animals are actually able to communicate with us on a readily ready basis!

I keep Peter the Rabbit on a glass lion container that I keep my medicines in. I have been prescribed about 17 different medicines from the brain injury and breakage that I had gone through in 2013 and I take them on a daily basis. My roommate goes with me to the VA Hospital to get them, then she brings them home and sorts them out on a day-to-day basis for me to take, day at a time, sorted out for three months at a time. Peter the Rabbit helps me to take my medicines on time, three times per day. He likes also when I eat. He likes the treats that I give to him. He isn't like George who only wants a lot of meat... Peter Rabbit likes vegetables and fruit and won't eat meat at all! He is such a good rabbit. He plays a solid game of snacks and asking for them in a nice and well-spoken and kindly fashion that I can hardly even describe it! "Ooh, Papa Krautant, what kind of fruit is that? Passionfruit, you say? Can I try some? Looks delicious!" he will say things like that to me. He does it for all kinds of vegetables and fruit that he hasn't tried yet, and because he is very young, there are a lot that he hasn't tried yet. But he will, watch. He will!

Peter the Lion is really young, too. I don't remember where I got him from, but his method of speech is really abbreviated. He starts out with a "whow, whow, whow, whow... what do you want to talk about papa?" Or he will bring up something good about the food, like the steak that I gave to George. Peter the Lion doesn't eat steak, though. He is a Vegetarian.

That covers the details about the other animals.

Now I shall go into what their conversation with me are like. Me and Krishna are going to have some conversation with them over the course of the next few days to put something down in this new book that I am writing about *The Elegant Lion Named George*.

We came back from getting shrimp to eat at the store and sat in the kitchen. I sat at the bench next to the cooking area and Krishna got to cooking. While she did, I asked her: "George is in the other room and he was asleep last night. I am wondering... would he answer questions I ask him about Perle and Peaches?"

"I don't know... what would you ask..."

"She would ask me if I understood what the question was, papa!" Said George. "So, what is your question?"

"Can't you guess that I am wondering what your opinion is of Peaches and Perle?" I said it absolutely so he could understand that that was the question.

"They are remarkable creatures! Capable of doing magnificent things to you and me and each other! I like them a lot! How do you think I think of them? Not rude, I hope!" George was well spoken.

"That is good. Do they tell you what mystical things they are going to do?" I asked.

"They don't talk to me about much. They are magical. They talk to each other in Unicorn Speak, they do. I can't

understand what they say to each other. It is in a language
I don't understand."

"A Magical Language that is ununderstandable?" I said.

"Yeah, that's it, papa! That's it! But it means something
because they finish in giggles and laughs! Whatever does
that mean? Something miraculous, that is what it means!
And they have come across and told me that they have
magical powers, too!" He was waving his hand around at
saying that.

"What magical powers do they have?" I asked.

"They can fly, without wings... they just fly! With
their minds! And their eyes! And their ears! They can
sense their elevation and manipulate it to a higher being!
That is what they do for fun and for problem solving
exercises!" George was speaking profoundly about THAT
one! I guessed that *he* wanted to fly, too!

I changed the topic. "Do you think that Perle and
Peaches would do something positive towards my health
if they were able to?" It was a serious question.

George took a second to answer, then he came on
with a calm tone: "They are Unicorns. And they were
made like me in your Honor. They will use their Unicorn
powers to do whatever they can to bring as many miracles
towards your well-being that they can... and they will do
it straight to you and readily! They speak English! They
will talk to you about the methods of well-being!"

"All-righty, George. Thank you for the input. You are an excellent Lion. That is why I have named this book The Elegant Lion Named George!" I really liked telling him that and getting his opinion.

"That is what you called the book about me, papa Krautant? That is fantastic! I deserve no such thing from you! Elegant! That is a real term for a nappy and strappy lion like myself... with maty hair and a rough coat. But that is what you think of me? Thank you papa thank you!" George was all smiling and extremely happy about the judgement. But it didn't change his opinion. He still thought he was nappy. And he was... his hair over his head had been tangled up and got all stringently rubble and, well, nappy!

That concluded that part of that conversation. I departed from Krishna and went back into my room to write this story. Soon I shall ask George to tell me about the Peters.

When I was riding with Krishna to the burger joint to get something to eat, I asked Krishna to tell me what George thought about Peter the Rabbit. She said, in George's voice: "Pops, why do you keep on asking Krishna to speak up for me? What is wrong with you? Ask me to speak up for myself! That is what you should do!" George was irate.

"George, I tell Krishna to speak up for you because you put your voice through her voice and mindset. That is why I do it! I am still listening to you, you crazy Lion!" I was telling him the way it was. He should have understood, but he didn't. Perhaps he was just confused. I considered that to be a possibility.

George continued with his tirade, changing the subject. "Well, not only that but you don't even consider that I have a ding-a-ling or private parts. I am a ferocious lion! That is what I have! I belong with a penis! And I can use it, too!" George couldn't help but carry-on about it.

"George, your ding-a-ling isn't even visible! You have a seam of cloth because you are a Doll!" I knew he would be upset over me calling him a "Doll", but I wanted to get my point across to him. "You don't even HAVE a ding-a-ling!"

"Yes I do, Pops! I do! You just don't know it because you can't see it because it is private. It is hidden! And by the way..." he changed the subject... "do you like me to call you "Pops"? Or "Papa"? Or "Krautant"?"

"I don't like you to call me "Pops" because that is what Krishna calls her brother. I don't like it. Call me "Papa" or "Krautant". That should do it!" I was sound on that one.

"I don't like to call you "Krautant" ... that would mean Best Friends... but we have some issues sometimes. I will call you "papa" though... okay, Papa?"

"Ok. George, what do you think about Peter?" I asked him.

"I like Peter the Rabbit! He is an excellent creature! He is always so nice and pleasant to me! Even when he is in a bad mood, he doesn't say anything negative to me about anything at all! He is so nice! And Pete... he is..."

"Peter the Lion?" I asked.

"Yeah... Pete is his name! He is so friendly, all though he is rough spoken. He burbles a lot. And he is a Vegetarian Lion. Go figure! How can that be... Lions are supposed to eat Meat! How can he eat just vegetables and fruit and such things? That is disgusting! I don't know how he can do it! But he sure is kind! I'll say THAT about him. For sure!" George liked to talk about the Peters. And he continued: "I also like Perle and Peaches, too! They are sooo nice! They say kind things to me on a worldly basis! It is clear that they are Unicorns! Sometimes when they have something that isn't nice to say they will say nothing at all. That is what Unicorns do! And that is really nice of them! Do you like my opinion of those four animals?"

"I like it, George, I like it a lot! It is so responsible of you to have those opinions!" I was happy to say it. Then we arrived at the burger restaurant. "That is fine, George. Oh, we are at the restaurant now. Time to eat!" I was hungry for a burger.

George was quiet after that. I thought he was going to say something about the burgers, but he didn't. The conversation was over for the time being.

I had forgotten that I had written about Peter and Pete's recommendations by George, so I asked him today what he thought about Peter and Peter. He said: "Who?"

"Peter and Peter, George, what do you think about them?"

"Who are you talking about papa?" asked George.

I was more specific. "Peter the Rabbit and Peter the Lion! That is who I am talking about!"

George responded to that with an answer similar to what I have written down already on the subject. I imagine you will be able to remember. It is really well written.

The conclusion finished with a compliment: "You are such an excellent papa; you are you are! I appreciate you for asking me about the Peters! They are excellent creatures, and the lion is kin of mine!" He was so happy!


We were eating dinner tonight, with Peter the Rabbit inside of the lion statue that I save my medicines in. We were eating steak, with asparagus and corn next to it. Now, Peter doesn't eat meat, so he didn't say anything about it. But he DOES eat asparagus and corn and he was so happy to taste it!

"Hey papa, what do you have over there? It looks deeelicious!" He said it all cheerfully and full of curiosity.

"It is asparagus and cooked corn, you Rabbit, you!" said Krishna.

Peter took it in hold: "Oooh! Can I have some? Can I? I want to taste it I do I do I do!" He stammered in excitement.

"Oh, Peter... hold on!" I needed to scoop it up.

"Pull him over my ways, papa!" Krishna wanted to put his face in the settling of asparagus and corn.

I sent him over to her, raising him upright out of the lion and handing him over to her. She put his face on the corn and he gobbled it up readily. He was delighted! And he voiced his opinion of the matter to us wholesale: "Papa! Krishna! This is so delicious I can't even say it out loud... my mouth and throat are filled with nutrients now! Yes, I say, yes! I'm full now. You can put me back in the lion." George was so pleased that he sounded superhuman with his rudimentary speech.

I put him back and saved a steak for later to eat, at 7 pm. That is what I do... I save food and snacks for 7 o'clock pm. George wouldn't mind, so long as I shared some steak with him. But Peter didn't eat steak, so there was no matter there!

I then went into my room and began to write. Thus, this was written to this point. Interesting, isn't it?

Krishna was making breakfast, and I was sitting at the counter. Suddenly, George began to speak through Krishna: "Hey papa," he asked, "are you going up to see Krishna's brother for his birthday? Are you seeing him?"

George was excited to ask the question. I felt bad at my response because it wouldn't make him happy.

"No, George, it is too far away for Krishna to drive." I tried to say it calmly.

"But papa, he wants to see you! I know this! Why don't you go!" George was getting obtuse at the negative answer I had given him.

Krishna spoke up: "Because I only have three days off of work, and that is not enough time to drive up there and back. It takes a whole two days for a trip up there and back. So, no, there is no time! And I need to save money to pay off my mortgage, too. So no, we are not going!" She was urgent in her speech.

"I don't like that Krishna; I don't like it at all! Why don't you fly up there?" George was really starting to feel down and aggressive. I was worried he would come over and start to bite us, yelling "Bring him to the house! Bring him to the house! OR TAKE THAT!" Bite Bite "And THAT!" Bite Bite. Something like that went through my mind. It was horrible!

"Because I don't make enough money to pay to fly, George," said Krishna. She was moving quickly, like she didn't want to have that conversation.

George changed the subject to the horrible comments he had been getting from me and Krishna: "Hey papa, are you going to write about this?" he asked.

"Why yes, George, I was thinking about it, somewhat. Why do you ask?"

"Because you are a really good writer, I think, as a Lion and a harbinger of Good Faith! And I think you should write down that Pops is 70 years old this month! That's what I think!" George was now well-spoken.

"George, I am not 70 years old!" I said. It was a mistake that George explained.

"No papa... I am not saying that YOU are 70 years old... I'm saying that POPS is 70... Krishna's brother is called POPS, not papa like you are! Man! What a foolish gesture you are! Foolish!" George was going off on me for that mistake! He was very knowledgeable but also very emotional and lost his mind from time to time with his rampages he went on!

"Ohh," I said, "I get you now George. That makes sense. No need to go any further with it..."

He hesitated and I could tell he was thinking of something to say, but he said: "Ok, papa; Thank you for the compliment!"

"Does that settle that?" I asked him.

"That settles that!"


We were having a conversation about Hell as put forth in the previous chapter... and George said that Perle and Peaches didn't say anything negative about the people in Hell. "What are their problems, man? Those oafs have

no concept of what is "right" and what is "wrong"! Why
do you listen to them carry on? I even asked Peaches the
following question: "Why do you think that the people
of Hell are good people. WHY? ARE YOU AN OAF?
WHY DON'T YOU GO TO HELL?!?" And Peaches
responded in a positive way and said that perhaps they
DID deserve to be punished for their badness. That
is what they deserve! I told her so! Go figure, right? I
figured that Unicorns would be far more upright than
that." George was rattling his cage with disappointment.

So, I asked him a question. "So, what do you think
about Perle? She's a Unicorn too!" I wanted an answer.

George responded: "That oaf said that at first she
didn't agree with Peaches. That is beyond a Unicorn to
do! And I told her so! So, she changed her story and said
that she finally came to see things from the same light
as Peaches and agreed with her... hesitantly. I think that
is horrible! She has no concept of "right" and "wrong"!
What is her problem? That would explain why she says
so many negative things to me over time during the time
that I have known her. There is something deficient
with her system or something! I know this for a fact!
SOMETHING DEFICIENT!" George was furious at
the question.

"Well, George, there is something to that. I am
sure they are seeing the good side of the conversation
as well as the bad side, and the probably think that a
different judgement could have been put into place. But

in-regards-to the people who did negative things to me…
there was no reason to do so besides GREED. They were
Greedy people who deserve to burn in fires!" I was solid
on that point.

George said something to that, an argument: "So,
why does Perle not get that point from you on the subject,
since you are an expert on the subject having lived through
it, but she doesn't take your side? She is a Unicorn! That
is supposed to be her job!"

"Perhaps she doesn't understand the consequences."

"Perhaps. I say "DAMN HER! DAMN HER!" That
is what she deserves!" George was feisty.

"Perhaps. I'll think about sending her away."

George hesitated for an instant, then said: "No,
papa, don't send her away. I like her anyways. Forget the
bad things I said about her. She is just confused, that is
all. Confused."

"Ok, George. Ok. Let it go, ok?"

"Ok, papa; I love you. Krishna too!"

"Thanks George. Thank you."

And that concluded that conversation premise.


Peter the Rabbit interrupted the conversation I was
having with Krishna tonight. "Papa, papa! It is horrible!
Help me help me help me!" Peter cried it out in his

normally fidgety and calm voice... which wasn't so calm anymore.

Krishna spoke up for him: "Peter, it is okay. Just let it go." Then she directed the conversation my way: "Peter was having a nightmare about MacGor. He had an image of MacGor charging over and killing Peter's sister dead. He was really upset over that. I am trying to calm him down from the nightmare." Krishna was speaking in calm and knowing tones, like she had seen that activity before. Where? I wondered.

"Oh mama, mama... neuf, neuf, neuf, neuf... it was horrible! *I could feel her pain going through me!* And he killed her! *MacGor killed her!* Why did he do that?" Peter was still upset. What Krishna had said to him wasn't going through yet.

Krishna corrected him: "Peter! PETER! Nobody has killed your sister! Give her a call on the phone and she will answer! *Calm down!*"

So, with that Peter somewhat believed her and couldn't put together a reason why she would lie about something so important, so he went over to the iPhone and pressed her number that he had memorized in his Rabbit head. And then he began to speak after it rang a few times. Then he hung up. "Whew, you are right, Krishna! My sister lives! That is a good thing! Horrible nightmare THAT was!" Peter was calmed down now and happy that he just had a nightmare... just a little disturbed over the fact that his mind could act so errantly.

George then spoke up all of a sudden: "Peter Rabbit, you are a fallen down Angel who deserves Hell! That is how you are acting... that is what you deserve and that is what you will get!" George was really speaking loudly with his yelling. It was inappropriate, I knew that, so I countered him...

"George, you have no idea what you are talking about! Peter had that nightmare because he cares for his sister! And he fixed his suspicion by calling her and confirming that she is okay! Maybe you should do the same! Don't get on Peter!" I was obtuse with him because he was really negative right now.

"Ok, papa. I'll do what you say. But stop saying Peter to me. He has done nothing but say bad things about you to me lately." George was now making up stories, and I knew it. He wasn't talking about Peter Rabbit doing it, either. He was talking about Peter the Lion, who he sits next to next to my bed during the day... for the most part. They are in a close relationship because they are both Lions and bred of the same cloth.

"You are talking about Peter the Lion, George! Peter the Lion... is that true? Did you actually say negative things about me to George? Tell me or I will beat you!" I was saying it with the potential of anger to get my point across.

"Mew mew mew... mew mew mew mew mew" said Peter the Lion, whimpering. "No, papa, I didn't say anything bad about you! I just said that you hadn't visited me in a long time. But I know that you looked at me this morning when you took George to the scooter to ride with your Service Dog. I liked that. That was enough for me to know that you haven't forgotten about me. That is the most important aspect of being around your room and in your life here. Understand? Mew mew mew... mew mew mew!" Peter was crying in his usual way, but he seemed to like telling me what he told me.

"I am glad you like my response, Pete. Can I call you Pete, to keep you separated in syllables from the name of Peter the Rabbit, without the Rabbit? Would that work for you?" I was trying to be pleasant with him and to make him feel original and excellent.

"Sure thing, papa! I would like to be called Pete. Let me say it again... P..E..T..E ... Pete. That works for me, papa! Go ahead and do it!"

"No problem, Pete. I am going to talk to George for a little while about the new chapter I am writing about him and me going to war in this book. It is coming along. Can I go talk to him?" I wanted to separate what I talked to him about here from the chapter I was writing about it.

"Sure papa go ahead! I hope it is a good conversation!" Pete was an excellent Lion. Even if he was a Vegetarian. Not expected among the characters of supposedly meat-eating lions, right? Not supposed to be Vegetarians, right? Wrong! Pete the Lion is not only distinguished, but he is also a Vegetarian! And he is proud of it, too! So there, you vicious beasty you!

I shall write about what George said in the part where I am having a conversation with him. I shall go there now!

Today I was sitting in the kitchen at the counter and Krishna was doing the dishes, when suddenly, out of nowhere Peter the Rabbit shouted: "Papa! Papa! I'm afraid! Help me help me help me! I just had a frightening nightmare about Mister McGor rising from the dead and coming over to me and beating me to a pulp! It was horrible! HORRIBLE! I can't rest now! Papa... do something about McGor. Can you do something to stop him? I don't know what you can do?" Peter was extremely upset and whining as he spoke. Poor rabbit.

"I can roll in and punch him in the face and knock him out!" I suggested.

"No, papa!" Chimed in George... "I will throw that fool to the ground for assaulting my kin and pummel him roughly into the dirt! I shall beat him until he is bleeding out of his eyes! I shall blast him with my strength to the downward realms of Hell where he belongs, and I shall leave him there blasted and beaten to bleed in pain and trauma in the deepest realms of Hell! That is what I am thinking he deserves... and that is what I shall do to him!" George was rambunctious in his statement!

"Yes George yes!" cried Peter Rabbit. "That is what should happen, and you are a Great Lion for coming up with that solution! I am pleased with knowing you! It is an honor!" Peter was extremely pleased that George was willing to fight for him...

"So, is that what McGor deserves?" I asked them, but I was sure it was.

"Papa, papa..." Peter cried out aloud to me, "McGor killed my mother and my sister! HE IS A VILLAIN! An uncouth monster! He deserves to be slain and put out of our hair! I hate that man! I HATE HIM! What George is going to do to him by pummeling him is what he deserves! He DESERVES to be SLAIN! That is what he has earned above all else! SLAIN!"

I answered him with what was accurate in my mind: "I agree with you, Peter... I really do. I am not making that up. I truly agree with you. It is my hope that we can meet McGor in Hell and punish him with pain and misery. After all, McGor is dead. That is what it said in the books and the news, so it is likely that he has already gone to Hell for killing your relatives. There is no other place that he could go to. He is an agent of Satan! That is who he is, and he is being punished in Hell for what he has done!" I had more to say about it - but I wanted Peter to give me his response first.

Peter said: "I am GLAD that McGor is dead! HE deserves Hell for what he did to my family! There is no respite for a person who kills a Rabbit! Especially a Rabbit kin group of a higher intelligence and who has humans as friends! What was he thinking, doing that? Nothing of worth! He deserves to be punished for those despicable murders he did!" Peter waved his arms side to side in anger and waggled his chin side-to-side in angst.

I responded: "God has made it clear to me that He is going to allow us to go to Hell when we die in a special roundabout way that prevents Satan or his demons or Fallen Angels from doing anything negative to us. And there, in Hell, we will come under the auspices of Jesus Christ and He will bring us into the counterpart of McGor so that we can punish him wholesale for a period of time for killing the kin of Peter! That is what McGor deserves, and that is what he shall get!" I was pleased with the answer, and it appears that Peter liked it as well!

"Ok, papa! We shall do it! I will take pleasure in being by Jesus's side there! He likes me, doesn't he? I think He does! Like you do!" Peter came over and gave me a hug. I hugged him back and noticed that his chin had stopped waggling around and his arms weren't flexing anymore.

And with that the conversation was over.

Krishna said to me tonight that she was going to make Samosas and asked if I wanted any. Peter responded: "Papa... can I try a samosa? They are made out of vegetables, aren't they? If so, that sounds deeelicious! If not, then I don't really want one with meat in it because I am a Vegetarian! So, which is it?" Peter was hungry and highly curious. He really wanted to try the new food we were going to eat. At least... it was new to him!

Krishna responded to him: "Peter, samosas are made out of buns and beef. You can't have any of the meat portion because, well, it IS beef! But we can peel out the beefy parts and give you a piece of the bun to eat... if you want..."

George interrupted: "Krishna and papa, you can eat the bun and I'll eat the beef! That is how it shall go, and that is what I want! So, that solves your solution. See... I am a problem-solving Lion, I am! What does that say about you two?" George was speaking really loudly.

"That puts that in order, it sure does!" I said to George. "Peter, I don't think we are going to take the buns off of the samosas, since George is going to eat the meat out of them... if we give you the buns then we will have no food for us? Besides, you are just a rabbit with a tiny belly. You won't even notice if you don't get any!" Peter was sad to hear that. He really wanted to get a bun after hearing George carry on about getting the meat and leaving us the buns.

Peter began to cry. "That is so unfortunate, pa- pa- pa- pa- papa! Why are you do do do doing this to to to meeee?" Peter sounded miserable.

I wanted to make it up to him... somehow. So, I tried the following: "Peter, I have changed my mind. Don't cry. I am going to give you some of the bun to eat. Not all of one, mind you, but enough to fill your tiny stomach up. That should please you. What do you think?" I was patient listening for an answer.

Peter mumbled and whimpered somewhat, then gradually began to stop. He mumbled to me: "Are you really, papa? That is so good of you. Sorry I was crying. It made me so sad that I wasn't going to get some. But I am okay now. Take me into the kitchen. Oh, wait...I am already in the kitchen. Forget I said that. Now, give me some vittles!"

"Ok, Peter. It is being made right now!" I told him.

A few minutes later the samosas were cooked and ready to eat. Krishna put some on a plate for me to eat and I was thinking about how to unwrap the casings from the meat within. I couldn't think of a way. So I told Peter: "Sorry my man, I can't give you any buns. I can't get them free of the meat to give them to you!"

Peter groaned. Then Krishna said: "That is true, Peter. Sorry, but you can't have these buns."

Peter was silent for a moment, then he said, in agreement with Krishna: "Ok. I get it. You can't give them to me. I understand."

"That is good Peter." Then I took another couple of bites from my samosa and wound up with a corner of the arrow that goes around the beef without any beef in it. So, I said: "Here, Peter... try his meatless portion. How does it taste?" I put it in his mouth and let him bite into it.

He groaned and stopped biting it after a taste: "Ooh papa... I don't like it at all! Take it out and finish it yourself!" He made a lulling noise like he was getting ready to barf.

Krishna spoke up: "I think he doesn't like it because it must taste like beef and Peter can't stand beef at all!"

"Is that why he sounds like he is getting ready to barf?" I asked her.

"It sure is! Give him some vegetables later and he will be okay. We have some in the refrigerator. That is what they are for!" Krishna was very adept and vociferous at giving thoughtful solutions to the problems we had. I told her so. "Thank you!" She said. And with that the conversation ended... for the time being.

I'll write more about those topics mentioned so far, a little bit later.


"Hmm... whadami gonna eat? What?" asked Peter the Rabbit. Krishna was in the refrigerator. She came up with some ideas.

She pulled out a bag of Sugar Snap Peas and mentioned it to me. Then she pulled out a basket of strawberries that looked quite tasty. "You can share these two snacks with Peter if you want! He will be happy and appreciative to you for it! So, do it and you both will be pleased!" She waved the two containers in front of my face and showed them to Peter then began to put them back in the fridge.

As she put them back Peter said in a happy voice: "Papa! I am so glad we are getting a snack! My belly is SO HUNGRY! What would it take to get something done to make it so that this interruption of my diet wouldn't happen again? Can you ALWAYS eat with me, papa?" Peter was curious but very nice in asking the question.

"Sure, Peter. I would have no problem with sharing food with a Rabbit. A Rabbit that is kind and nice and well-spoken, too! You are an excellent Bunny!" I was being happy with him. Because I was happy!

"Can we start eating them now, papa?" asked Peter.

"No, Pete, we shall eat them at the regular snack time tonight." I told him the time, and he Rogered-up that he had heard it.

"Ok, papa. I shall wait!"

So, we waited for about an hour and a half. Then I went in there and opened the raspberries and ate some. Then I gave some to Peter. He smiled and gobbled them down so fast that his belly filled up after the third raspberry. Man, Peter has a small stomach! But he is a remarkable creature *and I love him!*

I finished the raspberries and we saved the Sugar Snap Peas for another day. Peter was full and I didn't want him to rupture his belly eating too many goodies. So, I threw the basket to the strawberries away. Then I came back to the lion jar that Peter the Rabbit rested in daily and gave him a kiss over the brassy fibers that are stitched into his mouth. He was happy and kissed me back. To that he said "Remarkable!" It was, too.

And that concludes that conversation. There was one more that we had... but I have to wait until Krishna comes home to get an idea of what it is all about. She is at work right now, and I don't want to write down too much without her being present to say things on the Peter's or George's or Peaches's and Perle's behalf. She is such an intelligent lady that it defies description to put in the ramifications of her speeches on the animal's behalves.

So, I shall write no more about it tonight. I shall go elsewhere and write different stories in different avenues of this computer. See ya later!

I brought George into the kitchen and sat him next to Peter the Rabbit for a spell to eat some Turkey Jerky. Peter started out the conversation while I was taking the wrapper off the jerky. "Papa, thank you so much for the pickle you gave me today! You didn't have to do that!" He was very pleased. I could tell that he probably wanted more of it, even though he was full because the pickle was so big. And spicy! It was a HOT PICKLE! And I really enjoyed it. Peter kept on asking me for more, then would eat it rapidly with a "num num num num num num num" noise coming out of his jaw. Then he told that he was full and had eaten enough. "You can finish it!" he said to me unnecessarily. Unnecessarily because I would have eaten it anyways. Peter likes to fill the diatribe with whatever seems to fit without thinking much about the ramifications of the speech nodes.

I was done taking the wrapper off the Turkey Jerky. It was a small slab. I held it up for George and he came over to me immediately and launched his jaw around the meat of it. "Num num num num num num num... boy is that delicious! Num num num num num num num num num." I let him rest while I took a bite, then he hollered at me "give me some more!" So, I did, and he gobbled it down with a num num num noise again. Then I took a bite and gave him the rest of it. He gobbled it down. Then he sat backwards very pleased with me and himself. He was pleased for Peter, too!

"What is the nature of water?" said Peter the Rabbit to me. "I wonder about that all the time. Should I be drinking some of it?"

I tried to respond positively to him for asking such an easily answerable question. "Peter, you are a miraculous rabbit. I thought you were getting water to drink yourself out of the faucet. You aren't, I see now. That must change. Perhaps you are scared to walk over there and get it yourself. Perhaps. So, what is the solution?"

"Papa. I can't flex my arm enough to make the handle turn on! I tried and failed!" Peter was trying to counter my statement of being scared... which he obviously wasn't.

"Ok Peter. Then perhaps I shall start to bring the water over for you to drink out of my cup. That will do the trick! You should definitely be drinking the water we have if you can. Will you do that for me?"

"Ok, papa... I shall do it readily!" Peter wanted to drink the water. I could see that from a mile away.

I changed the subject then. "Say, Peter... George...

can you guys tell me what else I should write about you after our meeting?"

George answered first: "Write about how many special things I have done for you! Miraculous things! Miracles, I say again! I take such good care of you, both here and in the future! I have taken great care of you ever since we first met in the Hospital. I do things like move objects for you and speak through Krishna for you and transmit ideas to your head through space and time! I pray for you daily, both in the morning and at night... and I help you pray in your head when you are thinking about doing good things for people. Or when you are thinking about sending those villains who did the negative things to you in prison to Hell! And that is where they will go! So, what do you say about those recommendations?" George was then silent and waited for me to answer him.

"That is an excellent set of recommendations. I bet you don't even know what happened to my attorney for the prison sentence, do you? She was fired by the BAR for failure to listen to her clients, then she died. I was told in a book by Gary Sinise on a random page that the bitch has gone to Hell! That is where she belongs, for what she did to me!" I couldn't think of anything else to say to George and Peter the Rabbit then.

Peter answered second: "What George is saying about your remedies to well-being are accurate! It is my desire to do nice things to help your health move forwards and be good. I want you to be in excellent shape. I am sorry that you are so fat. Please don't get angry at me saying that you are fat... but you are! The medicines that you take are doing it to you. I can tell. But you are on a diet, and that is a good thing. For you to do and everything. That is all I have to say to you. Best of health to you. And... one more thing. I like to eat vegetables with you and fruit too! And I will gladly drink the water you bring to me... just start to drink more of it for my presence. Or iced tea will do, too... because it has no meat in it. I am, after all, a vegetarian!"

"Ok, Peter! Thanks for looking out for my health and eating the goodies that I give to you to eat! That is so kind of you to do, and I am very appreciative of it!" I paused for a moment, then I said to the two of them: "Now, I am going to leave the kitchen and go to my room and write down this excellent conversation we had with each other, all three of us. I remember what they are, and each of you can enter my mind at will and remind me of what to write about when I get to that part... okay?"

George and Peter both said: "Okay, papa!"

"Good night papa!" said Peter the Rabbit.

Then George said: "Papa, are you taking me into your room with you so I can sit next to the bed by your side while you are on the computer?"

"Sure, George. You can come with me anytime!" And with that I picked him up and brought him with me to the room, put him next to the bed by Perle and Peaches and Peter the Lion. I got on the computer, which was plugged in and opened my file on George the Lion. From there I began to write.

And here you go!

I was reading my book about Unicorns, (that is its title... Unicorns), on the page of Truth and mysteries and it said that a Lion borrowed a Unicorn's horn as a cane and the Unicorn gave it to him, then the obtuse Lion used the horn to kill the unarmed and innocent Unicorn. Horrible!

That leads me to thinking about how George says all sorts of negative lies about Peaches and Perle. They are both Unicorns, with horns and everything. And they are white Unicorns. They are wholesome and plentiful and graceful. There is something wrong with George, him feeling the need to say such negative lies about the Unicorns. That tells me that if he could and he had a horn of theirs, that he would kill them with it, too! I am going to tell them to avoid giving him their horns for any reason whatsoever.

Ok, telling them worked. They have taken my word for it and the readings from the Unicorn book that I had done... and they put it to solid criteria. They refused to say anything to George about it, so as not to disrupt him in any way. That worked out well. George didn't say anything bad about it or do anything that was rude. And he didn't try to take their horns off of their bodies, either. That was good of him! He was getting the criteria of the restrictions put upon him by ME, his master!

But he was still capable of refusing to obey them. So, I decided to keep an eye on him to make sure that he is not doing something rude to the Unicorns. He could say bad things about them and there was nothing I could do to stop him. Just so long as that was the limit of the bad things that he would do to them!

Peter the Lion got involved in the conversation later. He said: "Hey papa, can you put me and Peter the Rabbit and Peaches sand Perle into Medicare? Can you? What is there to stop us from being cared for? What?"

"Peter, you may not understand this because you are a lion and you fall under a different set of rules than the rest of us humans do. But that is the point. You are a Lion, and people in the United States don't put programs into Lionkind! It is illegal! If not, it simply isn't done! You have to be a human to get Medicare!"

"But I am a Lion, papa! That is higher in evolution than the human will ever be! So, why do they not want me to be on Medicare?"

I answered him wholesale… "Peter, it is because the Lion IS higher evolution. So, they don't catch as many diseases or have as many germs or even the case of getting viral infections like the humans do. Thus, they can't have Medicare because it plays no role in curing them for no illness because they don't catch anything… being Higher Evolved like they are!"

Peter the Lion responded a lot: "I have colds, papa! I

caught the flu and was coughing and coughing it up! That was an illness about me that was wholesale and negative! It was bad, papa... bad! Don't you believe me? What can I do to prove it to you?"

"You can't do anything to prove it to me, Peter. I haven't seen you sniffing or coughing or hacking it up at all since I have had you. That has been for the last six years, you fool! So, you show no signs of illness because you don't get sick! You are a healthy object with the rudiments of a genius! Whatever do you think it is... the flu? You retard! You can't catch the flu! You're too evolved!" I was trying to tell him the way it was, so as to end the seemingly erroneous conversation.

I said it in a steady tone of voice.

"Papa... you are right. I am evolved. I feel like I get sick, though. Is that just mental?"

"It is George. It is. Keep that in mind."

"Ok. Thanks, Papa! Thank you!"


"Sunshiney has something to say about your health, papa." George was now talking about the cat.

"What does she have to say, George?" I asked him because I wanted to know.

"She thinks that you are a blessed soul that deserves the highest praise among the believers of God, and it is a blessing from God and His Angels! That is to you, papa! And that is what the highly intelligent creature Sunshiney the cat is saying about you. Isn't that nice of her to do?" George was thrilled to say it. He was so happy that such a blessing was happening for me!

I responded with the same happiness: "George, that is such a remarkable blessing, I cannot even describe it! A blessing from God as spoken with magical powers through my roommate's cat! How remarkable is *that?* It is remarkable! Will I get special powers from it?" I wanted some special powers. It was a gift from God, so I figured that such a thing would have special gifts installed.

George answered kindly: "Special Powers is exactly what you are to be given, papa! Your health will remain excellent, you won't get sick, your cancer will remain inactive, and you will live a long and fruitful life! That is what is coming for you! Are you happy?"

"I am happy, George! Very happy! Thank you for the information! I think that God is an excellent Spirit and he does plentiful things for us creatures of the Earth! And everywhere if there are other forms of living creatures on other planets! Bless them all!" I was happy to say that to George, too!

"Ok, papa. I am glad that you see it that ways. Sunshiney is a good PrayerCat, isn't she?"

"She sure is, George. She tells it like it is, with prayer and meaning. She is such a good cat! Bless her soul!" I was glad to say it aloud. George really appreciated the compliments... even if they weren't directly to him and to one of his fellows instead. He still appreciated it.

That was all for that conversation. We went on to watching the Western Channel on TV.

"Papa, can you have some Sugar Snap Peas with me for a snack tonight? Can you papa? Can you?" Peter the Rabbit was talkative in a little way.

"Ok, Peter! We can have some at 7 PM, okay?" I responded.

"Ok, papa. Ok!"

Today I was sitting at the counter to the kitchen with Peter the Rabbit in the lion shaped cup that holds my medicines in it. My roommate Krishna was making me some expresso in the Breville coffee and expresso maker. She gave me a cup of it, and Peter asked about it. "Boy oh boy, papa... what is that? Is that a cup of expresso? I have never had a cup of coffee before! Am I saying that right... Coffee? I think I am! What does it taste like? Can I try some?"

I answered him resolutely. "It tastes very deeeelicious, Peter. I think you can try some. I am sure that you will like it, too! Here..." I moved my full cup over to his mouth and leveled the cup to allow the expresso to move forwards to Peter's mouth.

He drank it up, chugging: "Gulp! Gulp! Gulp! Gulp! ... boy papa, that is definitely deeeelicious! Can I have some more of it?"

"Sure, Peter... you can have some more until you are full!"

Peter tried some more, and then he pronounced that he was full... and that the expresso was a tasty concoction. "Papa, that is the most delicious elixir that a person or beast could imagine! What is it made out of? Beans.... Right? That is interesting! How can it be that beans can produce an elixir that is so delicious that it defies comprehension? How?"

"Peter, they grill the beans to turn them into a paste of bean-curds and then then heat them up and flow water through them... which pulls parts of the bean to the taste-function of the matter and thus puts the caffeine and other goodies within the mix. That is how it works! Interesting, isn't it?"

"That defies comprehension, papa! Good explanation of it, though. You are a miraculous producer of the coffee grounds! That is what you are! And I am complimenting you too, Krishna, because YOU were the one to make that drink. So... YOU deserve to get credit for it, too!" George was being really kind with his speeches. He did a miraculous job, I thought, too.

The conversation was off for about an hour. Then I opened my drawer into the box with the descriptions of where my presents for the days leading up to Christmas were. Within it was a paper that said to go look on my bed. I looked and on there was a container with olives that were made with almonds within them. They were in a syrup. I took them into the kitchen and said: "Thank you Krishna!" to Krishna. Then I opened up the container.

Peter said immediately: "Hey papa! Those are olives, aren't they? Can I have one of them? They are good for a Rabbit, aren't they? If they are good for me can I have one?"

"Sure Peter. Here... try one and tell me how it tastes." I held one up to his mouth so he could taste it.

"Glub Glub Glub Glub... boy, papa, those are tasty! They taste like a combination of sweet and bitter and sour and bitter again! What is that taste coming from?"

"It is coming from the almonds within it. Each one of the olives has a slab of almonds cut within it. Tasty, huh?"

Peter was highly pleased. "Very tasty, papa! Very tasty! They almost tasted better than the expresso did. Almost. But not quite. The expresso was divine! The almonds were a close second!"

"Thanks Peter. You are such an excellent Rabbit!"

"I appreciate it, papa! Thank you too!"


Another day I went to my gift location guide box and saw on a sign to check behind the carousel. So, I looked there and there was a bag with a device in it. Krishna told me to be careful, so I was. I moved the bag over to my sitting area in the kitchen. There, on the counter, I pulled the device out of the bag. It was a little bitty drinking glass with Peter the Rabbit's stencil on it, bolting from side to side! And there was a little dish that came with the drinking cup, that had a saying in handwriting on it that said something about Peter running really fast to evade the enemy and to make his way home along the old fir-tree! Very nice! It was a coffee-cup for my expresso! I had a batch inside of it the next day. It was delicious and had the taste of Peter's stencils tasty along the edges of it! Funny!

It was such a delightful present! It gave me the presence of Peter in the stencil of him on the cover of the cup and the writing about him running free! That was a solid presentation and an excellent present. It is divine that Krishna knows and pays attention to the onsets of the creatures of Peter, both the rabbit and the lion, so that she gave determine the kind of and get me the relevant presents regarding those creatures. And delightful creatures they are! I really enjoy the present... and it gave me something nice to write about the Peters and the presents about! Nice!

Today is Christmas Eve, and we will be opening presents in an hour from now. Then we are going to dinner at a local Steak Restaurant in town. The name is kept secret because I don't want to have to get permission from them to put their name in a book... so I have kept their name private. But they are a steak restaurant. Delicious! We shall be getting treats there and dinner after we open the presents. Then Krishna's brother has a work-related segment to go to for Christmas, so he will depart to go there. It is in a different city. I could be mistaken, but I think he needs to fly there in an airplane. Doesn't matter. He will be gone for Christmas. But he will have gotten his gifts before then.

But that does it for this Chapter! This chapter was about the Peter the Rabbit and the Lion and the two Unicorns named Perle and Peaches. It has been a thorough chapter, with details all the way across it. It has finished with the divine present I have gotten for Peter the Rabbit. So, the chapter is now over, and it is time to write about other elements of my raising and enduring the remedies of George the Lion! Remember, this book is mostly about HIM! So, that does it for this chapter. Enjoy yourself reading the rest of this book!

Actually, that does NOT finish this chapter! What I haven't put in here yet is how the animals have been receiving money from Krishna for spending on my birthday. How much has been saved so far? $40! Who received it?

George had a total of eleven dollars, plus another four that he got from Kinesha from the goodness of her heart to me. As Krishna and I were standing around, Peter the Rabbit came out and said to us: "Mama, papa, I don't have enough money to give papa much for his birthday. I only have five cents!" He was so sorry for it. He was genuinely apologizing.

Then Peter the Lion whimpered: "blunt blunt blunt blunt! I am so sorry! I don't even have that much. All I have is one cent! How can I save some more money for papa?" He was sorry too. I thought about it for a moment, then asked Krishna the following...

"What do the other animals have in their savings for my birthday?"

"Well," Krishna said to me, "Sunshiney has a total of five dollars! I know... that is a lot of money! But Peaches and Pearle... well... they are unicorns and they don't save money or even accept donations. They are planning on using Magical Powers to Create a brand of Gifts for you to have, papa! What do you think about that? They are unicorns, after all... so they have that Magical Power!"

I questioned her further. "What about Forest and Paige? You have addressed a few of the animals. What about the rest of them? The remaining two? Forest and Paige? They are intelligent animals, they are. What is their take on the issues of rewards for my birthday?"

Krishna was resolute in her response! "Forest has a total of ten dollars for your birthday! And Paige? Guess how much she has... ten dollars herself! That is a total of about forty dollars total! Nice, huh, papa?"

"That is excellent, Krishna! I am so glad that they have received so much money for my birthday! So divine, it is it is!" I was extremely pleased with the numbers. And the animals were excellent in character and divine in organization. I really appreciated them, I did!

# CHAPTER 3

## THE GENETICS OF GEORGE/ A COMBINATION OF SPACE AND ENERGY AND TIME

There is something to be said about an animal that put itself into Creation at the whims of a Veteran who had been a victim of murder. George was put into Creation upon the recovery of the Veteran in the hospital. There must have been some semblance of knowledge that went before the Veteran to the animal to present him. And he has a full personality, so there were copies of the Veteran's mind that went along with it in the Spell of Being. And there was something to be said about the movement and process of the forces of thought that went into the animal's actions. He was borne with the ability to portray thoughts and actions through a third-party person that was somewhat related to the Veteran. And the question is this: what does it know about the tactics of the Veteran of Special Operations Capable in the military? It must know something about that, too!

Another question is this: what is in George's DNA... if he even HAS any DNA? What is it in the putting-together of the ions of his materials that makes him have such an ability to be present in the mind of a person without entering their body? How does he have the ability to progress his thoughts to another person so that they can speak for him, even from a distance of rooms away? How does such a thing happen?

And yet another question has to do with what will happen when the Veteran dies. I am quite religious... a Christian, Muslim, Jewish, Hindu, and Buddhist altogether... and I believe that when we die, we go to the Hereafter, where we are Reborn. Eventually, our animals and pets come with us, and that means that the dolls that have come to life in my presence come with me. Don't believe me? What do you know about death? Only what you are told. The Hereafter exists in a realm of space and time that defies the current exhibition of space and time as we know it. It defies them and exists in the realm of Heaven and Hell, separated. It is a fixation place to determine which place one is going, to Heaven or to Hell. And your animals and pets have followed suit with your behavior on this earth so that they will belong with you wherever you go. So, it makes sense for a Veteran in

George's existence would do things to bring themselves
closer to him. Even if that means that they will be
"Speaking to a Doll to make it happen". Those things
get put together and seen in the Hereafter by a Force
that is subliminal and pervades all sense of knowledge
and know-how. That is what I believe, and that is the
reason why I do what I do with George and my other
animals in mind.

So that raises the question of this: what Forces of the
Universe were responsible for the Creation of a Lion like
George? Let me tell you my theory...

There is a combination of Space and Energy and
Time that plays into the onset of the properties of the
Creation of George the Lion. They play a lot into the
science of things.

For starters, what makes up a Soul? George has a
Soul... it is what allows him to have a language without
having the physical characteristics of speech organs in his
body. His mouth is a stitched-shut perusal of cloth and
fibers. Now, by definition, the term "PERUSAL" means
to read... so by my putting it in the statement it shows
that George is CAPABLE of reading in my mind... even
with a no-holds-held mouth. His Soul understands what
words are and the sounds and syllables they make. And
his Soul understands how it is that the average person
with a mouth and throat is able to talk and make sounds
that make sense to others. Thus, because George's Soul
understands how such a human throat and mouth works,

his Soul is able to put forth a frequency that leads to "words" in the mouth of a human. That is a magical Spirit nature of George.

George was built around the idea of helping me out when I was disabled from being a victim of murder. His Soul used my items of intelligence (I am really smart) and my ability to speak in large words to his advantage in putting together a means to communicate to me, as a Doll, but one that has the magical capabilities of transferring thoughts and powers of verbs and nouns to the mouth of my roommate Krishna so that she can speak for him. People would say that I am insane doing it and listening to it as if the doll was actually speaking... but let me explain this to you: George is not a Doll... George is a Lion! And a fierce one at that! He has vowed to protect me from any onsets of negativity from bad people... with death to them if necessary!

That is a distinct knowledge that comes from the ideas of the onsets of the positives and negatives that surround life of a person. A Lion is different, though. They are built differently than a person is. For example, they have 4 legs and no arms. But George, even though he is a lion, has two arms and two legs... like a person. He is a mixture of the two species. That is magic how that happened. To think about it, some designer in a shop drew a diagram of George with the idea of making a skin around him surrounding a stuffing with colors and textures and shades in the skin on the outside so he can appear to be alive. And what isn't known about it is that his design structure... the thoughts that they had in his or her head when they did it, we such that they modified the structure of the Forces of nature around the George Lion in such a way as to make such things like the transmission of light rays with thought become apparent, and the transmission of thought though the changing of the onset of Gravity also became apparent... thus allowing George to give a human person... Krishna... the ability to portray his ideas in speech in his voice become apparent and regular. Thus, the science of the matter works in the regular science that is known to us! It just isn't apparent until one thinks of it!

Now I shall go on with discussing the onset of Light and how that plays into the Creation of George the Lion.

Light plays a big part into the Creation of George the Lion. Somehow there needs to be a way for the molecules of thought to move from George's head to the head of Krishna, and to do so in such a manner that they can be made into words and deeds thought and portrayed to others with speech by Krishna. That has to do with the molecules within the brain doing certain things to space and time that flies in the face of the known physics that we are aware of right now... unless someone else has written about such a thing occurring before! Either way, that leads to a multiple method for portraying what has occurred with George's thoughts and speech.

I shall explain how the light omitted from the mind of George projects a ray through space and time to the mind of Krishna. Then the light rays project through space and time to the mind of Krishna and the flow of the photons projects the ideas of George through the brain cells of Krishna to the nucleus and electrons of the cells.

The onsets of light play a huge part in the flow of thoughts from George's Lion mind to the brain cells of Krishna. The flow of electricity plays a great deal into the makings of the movements of the brain cells of Krishna by flowing through space and time in a way that is normal for light to flow. They put forth a force within the cells of the brain of Krishna in such a manner as to change her thoughts to something similar to what the message is to get across, to putting forth thought-waves that procreate the verbiage of George through Krishna, to playing a minor miracle of brain wave patterns that allow for the onsets of the thoughts and Creation of miracles throughout the process of normal existence. One that accelerates the miracles and makes them thus more likely to occur. Those are tall orders of existence happening through the mental abilities of George, the Genius Lion that knows no limits!

Then again, I may be wrong about there being no limits to George. Today he was watching TV with me in Krishna's room on her bed and a commercial came onto it. George asked me: "Papa? Do I need to be put on Medicare?"

I thought it was an obtuse question. "George, you are a Lion! You don't get sick to where you even *need* Medicare! What are you thinking of?"

George was reactive: "I NEED IT BECAUSE I GET SICK, PAPA! I need the care from it!" George was getting upset with my answer.

"Don't get upset, George. Don't get upset!" I plead to him.

George took a second to think, then another idea came out of his head: "Papa, papa... I have COPD. What am I supposed to do about it?"

I was astonished, and curious. "George, I don't even know what COPD is or what it stands for. What is it?"

"Cardio-Obstructive Pulmonary Disease! I can't believe you didn't know that! My lung gets obstructed and I can't breathe right!"

"George, I don't see that in you at all! I think you only have it in your head. Your breathing is totally normal. Why do you come up with such oddities?"

"You don't see my lung as breathing oddly??

"No George, I don't!"

George got excited. "Oh. Thank you thank you thank you, papa! That is so nice of you to say to me!"

I was glad that George liked it. I didn't like him thinking that he was sick when he wasn't sick, or diseased when he wasn't showing any signs of disease. And besides, he was a Lion. He wasn't to succumb to the same sort of sicknesses that the rest of us humans had to sustain.

The real question I had was this: What elements of Science regarding Space and Time are you going to come up with the idea that you had COPD? That was the question I had for him. So, I asked it.

George responded by answering the question! "My lungs have a symbiosis of movement within them that fluctuates when there is an oddity. And in the air in space and time around me there are molecules of matter that flow within them! So, what do they do? I'm asking you! What effect do those particles have on the cells of the body?"

"I don't know, George. They change the flow of the movement within them, with their presence, I think." I was only guessing. He seemed to be making a point.

"Their force of Gravity makes the particles within the cells move around all oddly, from time to time, and the flow of time, which can move backwards, makes it so that the movement can be in bizarre directions! That is what it does! IT CREATES DISEASES! It makes the lungs put out molecules of matter that interrupt the airflow by molecules of air within the atmosphere. That is where the pain comes from! The lack of breathing! It is from the molecules of the air being disrupted!" George was speaking with a loud voice and he was using big words. He was putting his intelligence to the fullest scale of being.

I responded with some criticism to what had said.

"George, I realize that with your intelligence you can see things happening that the average person cannot tell. That is true. But the onset of COPD within you? I don't see it. You have not had an interruption of speech or breathing that I could tell at all within the course of the last six years that I have had you. It you had a COPD problem, then your breathing would have been interrupted! So, it is NOT INTERRUPTED! You are MAKING IT UP! You are *not sickened* by COPD at all! You breathe totally normal!"

George caved into the tone of my voice. "OK! OK! I believe you papa! Sheesh! No need to be so rude! Darn it darn it darn it! I wanted you to believe me! I tried and tried! Why can't you believe me papa? Why not? I FEEL like it is making me SICK! What is wrong with me?" George asked the question honestly. He was very disturbed.

"George, you know what a person is that says they are sick when they are not? They are called a "Malingerer". That is what you are. You don't have COPD. You aren't even ill. But you are a Malingerer. That is the sickness that you have... making up that you are sick. Stupid Lion!" I called him out for it. He was sad now. He pouted.

"I hate you papa! I hate you! YOU make me sick! *YOU DO!*" and he pouted and pouted. I left the conversation at that and ended the continuing diatribe. I figured I would interact with George again later, after he calmed down some.

It was a while.

"Papa, do you think I could ride in a buggy?" George had come around to asking me bizarre questions again.

"George, there are no buggy's down here. They are in the Western Show on TV. They don't even exist like that anymore." I was trying to drive him to common sense.

"But I want a buggy, papa! I want the horses to pull us around and to put us into steam with the makings of a horsey engine! That is what I want to do!"

"No, George. What did I tell you? No such buggies exist anymore!"

"Darn, papa! So, what am I supposed to say to that? Do you want me to tell you about God? That is the next question I have. Who is God? What is His last name? Does He have one?" George was changing the subject to a religious one that he didn't have a lot of answers to.

"George, God has no last name. His full name is God!" I hoped that answered the question.

"So, His name is God. So, what does He do? Play the violin? What?"

"He is the God, the Man in Charge, the ebullient makings of a hero, the source of Goodness in the Universes, a great man, and an operator in the realm of the Spirit. That is what He is… a Spirit of Goodness!" I tried to explain it in terms that George would understand. He knew my language, so I figured that with his intelligence he would gather the meanings of the terms.

"God has told me to say a prayer for you, papa." George was showing his understanding. "He wants me to pray for you. He says you do remarkable things for the people around you. You are a giver and a kind hero. You are a legend! What are there that you want to do for the people around you? What do you want to do for Krishna? For the preacher? For her brothers? What do you want to do for those folks? The pleasure of such a gift shall be granted to you by God... just say the word! And He will deliver!" George put a pause in it and gave the statement time to settle in.

I responded in kind. "Thank you, George. The wishes are well-founded. Thank you for interpreting the commands of God to me! It is great that you understood them! So, tell me... what can you think of that those people want or need?"

He told me. I am not going to write about it here because it is private desires of private people. But he told me what they desired, and thus gave me the ability to pray for them to occur to God Himself!

And the behaviors of God can fall outside the realms of Space and Time. Time can move in any direction under the rulings of God. Space has rules that can be broken. The whole universe may not really be set up the way that we think it is. We can only tell by the settings of the light that projects through the universe. But the laws of physics within different places of the universe may operate differently on the photons of light rays. We don't know because we go by laws of Earth... not the rest of the Universe.

"Papa," said George, as we were watching Gunsmoke on TV; "I want to have a firearm! Give me a pistol and let me shoot it like Marshall Dillan does!"

I had to respond with the facts! "But George, you are going to get a pistol from the city by the military base for bringing with you and I to War! And it will happen soon! You will have it in your hands to shoot at the enemy!"

"I WILL, papa... I WILL? That will be excellent! I am going to shoot it and shoot it until the cows come home! (But I am not going to shoot any of the cows!)"

"That is good, George, but can I ask you a question? Can you keep it secret from Krishna? We don't want her telling you to fire the weapon in the house or around people who you don't know as enemies or anything like that. Can you make that assurance? Can you? I want it to be quiet! That doesn't mean that you and I won't be able to go to war with each other. It just means that there will be a silence and hesitation in speaking about it to others. Besides the enemies. Them, we will shoot!" I had wanted to give him a full summary of the subject matter as seen by my in my head. I succeeded!

But not immediately.

"But papa!" George was emotional. "I want to say things about shooting! I will say it on a day-to-day basis, I will I will! What is wrong with that?"

"What I have already explained is wrong with it, George."

"But why can't I just say the things I want to say and leave it at that?" George was running out of things to carryon about.

"Because it is wrong of you to get Krishna to say thing that will make you do something negative with your firearm."

George came to understand then. "Ok, papa, ok. I see what you are talking about. Just think about it. You had to tell me to stop talking by using words and lingo to explain it. Isn't that the same thing as saying things about shooting to Krishna? I don't understand the difference. But I understand the concept. I won't talk about shooting AT ALL to *ANYONE!*"

"That is good, George. But let me explain the concept of why what I said doesn't equal what you said. Is that okay?"

George accepted it. "Yeah, papa, that is okay. Continue."

I started out by going to a relevant topic… "What is told to us about the DNA inside of your cells, George? I know that they are very small and virtually impossible to see, but there is a science about them, isn't there? So, does the status of your DNA interpret the ideas that you get about things, in relation to how they are grounded on reality? Or does your DNA just "sense" things that make no sense or meaning? Which is it?"

"My DNA senses Reality, I think!" George was certain about that.

"I agree. So does mine! But there are interpretations within the definitions that occurs. The interpretations must be correct. Sometimes the effect of the reasoning defies common sense. That is because there are things that happen within this universe that are different than the interpretations that we have put in there with experimentation and science! They are different! How can I tell?" I left the question open for him to begin to draw an answer.

"It is a thought pattern that arises from the working process of your brain! And your brain has more cells in it than there are stars in the universe... that is how! Our thought process is a conglomeration of ideas within our brains! They flow within the many cells of the brain with the special powers of quarks and such defining them! That is nice, yes?" George was very illustrative with his answer. And he was correct!

"So, George, that makes us as creatures capable of understanding the higher characteristics of nature and the existence of special powers therein, right?" I wanted to make that clear to him. It was.

He answered: "Indeed! That is exactly how it works!

You have helped to illustrate the cause of it, papa! Thank you much!"

"No problem, George. It was my pleasure!"

George has put me in extremely good health. He has that honest prediction of Well-being from the structure of his well-defined DNA. What is it about George's structure that made him so excellent? Was it his making in a semblance to MY structure, bringing into his construction the steadiness of my Force Recon body? The wavelengths that went through the matter of the stuffing and the skin and the colors upon George's body and face and hair were so profound that they made the construction of his DNA that of a Genius! The question is... how do the wavelengths flow in a way that effects the atoms of DNA? That is the question I shall answer next.

The numbers of the mathematics of the wavelengths of light involved in the put-together of DNA defies common sense. Besides, the wavelengths of light are too small to measure. What then is the measurement to be used for determining light wave proclivity? What? There is no method mathematically inclined. So, how is it supposed to be done? What technique is used?

There is none that doesn't defy common sense.

"But you can tell me something, papa. Is Paige a thief?" George wanted to know if she met his definition. "Is Paige a vagabond?"

I answered him resolutely. "No George, Paige is NOT a vagabond. What draws you to such an odd conclusion?"

"But what about when she steals Forests food? What do you call her then?" George was Quizzitive.

"Oh... well... I guess you would call her a vagabond..." I didn't know what else to say.

George then intervened, changing his story! "I take it back! Paige is NOT a vagabond! She is a kind and excellent Service Dog! She obeys all your Commands, too! What an excellent Dog!" George likes to talk about her kindly.

I showed George that I liked his remarks: "That is so good, George! It is so nice that you make such pleasant comments about the excellent Service Dog!"

"Glad to hear it, papa! You make me so happy with your divine comments! And I am complimenting you papa because Paige likes it! Yes, she does!" George was very pleased with the outcome of him changing his story.

That was an indication of the makings of George's Deoxyribonucleic Acid (DNA)! It was structured so that it would recognize the differences between accepted speech and behavior and unaccepted ones and thus separate the two from each other. Thus, George was able to say things that ran counter to the negative thing he said without there being any error involved. And it would be accepted by the other person as being something of a higher order! Very nice the way he did that!

How is it that DNA can be built to sense the

differences between the positive and negative elements of behavior? What is it about the structure of the atoms that compose and hold the DNA within that allows for such a distinguishing aspect? I know that it is partly in the cells of Memory within the organism that distinguishes between the actions of others. The senses play a big part in it, and the capability to tell what the senses are determining plays a factor in it. And the memory can also have a part of it that has rehearsed doing, in and of itself, in the memory, at least, the rehearsal of doing the same or a similar negative thing that is being done to it. So, the memory can understand what it takes to do such bad things... at least in part. I know. I have been a victim of murder... and during my recovery I have tried to figure out what was going through the murder's heads while they did it. I don't know for sure... I just rehearsed what would happen if we changed shoes during the incident. It was horrible.

That doesn't mean that I would do that to someone else. I just think that I understand what the people who did it have going through their heads when they did it. Stupid.

But George is really smart. He asks me questions about my intelligence. Last night, he asked me: "Papa, I think that you are really smart! You have an excellent IQ that falls in the top realms of knowing. You know all sorts of things about science and technology and computers and the military and shooting and even injury and recovery. You know something about ALL of them!

That is a definition of Really Smart! Don't you know that? I bet you do! What do you think about what I said about your intelligence? Do you like it? I bet you do!" George was quiet then, taking in the meaning of his sentences and the solid answer that I gave to him.

"I like it a LOT, George! Thank you for the compliments! And you should know, those compliments were also made for you! You are a GENIUS, George! You are designed after me and you have the same capabilities that I do! So, what do you think about *that?*"

George was ebullient! "I like it papa! I like it a lot! A LOT! Thank you thank you thank you! You are a hero in my eyes! So is Krishna! She is a heroine too! Cheers!" And with that George grabbed a glass of Eggnog and drank some of the tasty spirits!

"What did you eat, papa? I can smell the vittles in your stomach and man-oh-man, do they smell delicious! What were they...papa? Tell me tell me!" George was highly curious about my vittles and he wanted some!

"George, they were quite tasty! I had Lamb Tikka Masala! You eat lamb... right? So, you should like some of the leftovers! That is what I think!" I was trying to please George.

"That would be good... papa! And I will gobble down those delicious vittles! Yes... I WILL I WILL!" George was excited!

"That is good of you, George. What else do you have to say?"

"I have a question, papa! A question! Is Pops coming by for Christmas? Is he? I hope so I hope so I hope so! I really like Pops and most of all his taste in Excellent Vittles!" George was divine in his pleasure bringing up the subject. Pops was a pseudonym for Krishnas brother.

Krishna answered him: "Yes, Pops is coming for Christmas and New Years! He shall bring presents with him!" She was thrilled!

George responded: "Are the presents going to come from Santa Clause? Are they, huh? He likes to use his elves to make gifts for the Good people to do Good things with! That is what they are for... a roadwork to Heaven!" George has the clause down pat!

I complimented him: "That is a distinct treatise you put forth, my Friend you George... you! I am very pleased with you!" I was so happy!

"Good to hear it, papa. Wow... papa sounds like Pops. Are you two twins?" George was curious and couldn't keep the question from me and Krishna.

"No, George... we aren't even related!" I tried to give him an accurate and determined answer.

"You're calling it out, papa. So, you two have similar names... so what? That means nothing, really. Nothing besides that Krishna may have thought the both of you as being friends and thus gave you similar names. That is it!" George was making a definitive depiction of what was occurring.

I appreciated his speak over.

"Papa," said George, "can I have some of your Bundaberg?"

"That depends, George... what do you want it for?" I asked him.

"Because the whippersnackle that I had before was too sweet! The lemonade man! The lemonade!" George fixed the altercation with him making up words.

I answered him in kind: "that's a good idea, George! I shall give you some of my Bundaberg when I go into the kitchen to drink some, ok?"

"Okay papa! Thank you thank you!"

That was a resolution of what George's DNA was all about. Eating snacks and treats! Drinking savory goodies! And the likes of things!

George's DNA has a realm of "Do Not Ask, Do Not Tell" within it. It drives a person to not speak to George to interrupt the worries of being seen as being insane! That is my Krishna is not responding in George's voice to anything right now. He two brothers are over at the house. And because she doesn't want them to think that she is "insane" saying things that a doll would say if it was intelligent (which George IS!). So, she is playing the "Do Not Ask, Do Not Tell" card and saying nothing in his voice at all. That is making it really had to write about George's take on the Christmas Season! And today is Christmas Eve! And today we are scheduled to go into the Steak Restaurant for dinner, and George is supposed to get some of the steak for a snack! I don't know what to do, because Krishna is refusing to say anything about George before her brothers for fear that they will just call her Insane! So, how am I supposed to feed George if we are going to eat with Krishna's brothers? How?

Not only that, but what am I going to do when they read over this book and think that I am insane? But then again, maybe they will read this part of the book and think that I am just making it up so that they won't get that supposition? Perhaps?

Yeah... I'm just making up this part of the story. It isn't real. Forgetaboutit.


It is toothbrushing time at night on the 21st and I am thinking of the gift I got tonight. I got a limitless cup that has a picture of Peter Rabbit stenciled on there, with his name. The cup comes over a plate that say something like: "Peter Rabbit had the desire to run fast and hard home to the willow tree!" It was a divine poem and it made Peter Rabbit sooooo happy!

Now it's Christmas Eve and I have received all my presents! From Krishnas brothers I got two tubs full of different types of tasty snacks. They also gave me two gift cards to the Coffee Shop where I write books. Krishna enhances the gifts with a full calendar for my wall. She also added multiple gift cards to eat at the restaurants in town... at least the best ones!

Then we went out to a steak restaurant to eat dinner. We left Paige and George at the house because it WAS Christmas Eve and there were a ton of people there! The food was delicious and tasty. Krishna and her two brothers and I all went. Afterwards, we drove home and went into the house and got some Pecan Pie that Krishna had made for us to snack on. It was delightful! We had Martinelli's grape juice beverage with it. Krishna had left it in the freezer in the containers that carried them so that they were mostly frozen. So, Krishna had to jiggle the containers to put out a burble of foam on each cup. It was drinkable anyways.

Then Krishna's brother went into the other room, and Krishna called me by name over to her room. When I got there, she whispered to me that George had gotten me a gift and he wanted me to go get it. George was laying on Krishna's bed from yesterday. He had a stomach that was partially filled with steak from his magical confluences with mine. When I eat, he gets full sometimes. That happened tonight because I was thinking about George at the steakhouse. For the snack that George got for me, though, he said to me: "Sorry it is so small, papa... it is the whole 50 cents that I had to spend on it. Sorry! I hope it is enough. And I must be quite so Krishna's brother doesn't sense us talking, right? So you like it?"

I tried the turkey-made pepperoni that was in the wrapper. It had been placed in hiding under the little pillow on Krishna's bed. I grabbed it and unpackaged it and took a bite. It was delicious! I ate the whole thing, bite for bite without missing any of it, and then told George how I liked it. "George, you definitely got your money's worth here with this divine treat! It was absolutely deeeelicious! And tasty, too! I want to give you a reward for giving me such a fine treat!"

George was appreciative. "Thank you papa! Thank you! I want you to know that it is in my DNA to be appreciative to you when you say such kind things about me! It does me a service, the kind messaging, and it makes me heal and be a ready healer of YOU, papa! I want you to know that! And it is in my DNA to use my language skills to tell you things about my DNA that make a lot of sense to a person who has the knowledge of how the Deoxyribonucleic Acid works and what it is composed of! That is something that I want to study more of... what DNA is composed of! Interesting, to say the least... right?"

I was appreciative back. "George, I am glad you are telling me such distinct ramifications of DNA that go far above and beyond that told to the average human. Keep it up, you Hero of mine! And above all, thank you so much for getting me a delicious treat with your 50 cents that goes far above and beyond what a person can afford! You have saved well, George! Let me know if you need any help saving again... and I will give you some money to buy more things!"

"Thank you, papa, thank you! It is my wish that you get the best of things I can get! I only wish I had more money so I could have gotten Krishna a gift as well... but I had no money left! So, I didn't get her anything! Can I next time?"

"That would definitely be acceptable, George!" Krishna was speaking now. "You didn't need to get me anything. Your company was worth millions. Millions!"

"Thank you Krishna! You are my Heroine! You and papa are both Heroes! Both of you are!" George was so happy with us. I could understand that he had had a delightful and ebullient Christmas Cheerful Episode. It was my hope that George would also have a wonderful New Years!

George has told me today that he is thinking about my birthday. "Oh yeah?" I asked him, "What are you planning on doing for it?"

George's answer was resolute! "Papa, I am going to buy you some solid gifts! Plenty of them! Think I am too broke to afford them? Guess again! I've got a resource for my money! Can you guess what it is? It's Krishna! She is going to give me money for getting you presents for your birthday! What do you think about THAT?"

"Oh wow, George... that is delightfully excellent! Are you gonna get more than the 50 cents that you had for Christmas?" He said he was getting a lot. But how much? A dollar? A dollar fifty? How much was he expecting from Krishna?

"A TON more than 50cents! I shall be getting you present after present! I'll be able to afford them, too!"

I was very pleased. "That is so good to know, George! I think that you will really enjoy getting me presents for my birthday! Did you know that birthday gifts are a thanks and celebration for the Creation and Existence of the receiver? I am so happy for your giving, George! Thank you for them!"

"That's good to know, papa! It is delightful that you can give me such a resolute example! Thank you thank you! You're excellent!" And that concludes the conversation.

The conversation was about how events that have to do with the Creation of a person involve the makings of light and space and time. It is about how the effects of that Creation involve differences within the laws of physics for the person involved. And if one considers that Time may not flow the way the average person thinks, but it may actually move sideways and backwards too, then it makes sense to think that people's souls may have existed in time and space before they came into being with "existence". They were alive and living before there were even bodies for them to live in. That is what the religious term "Spirit" means... on a religious basis!

The center of George's DNA are the elements of his Soul! And he has a distinctly excellent Spirit that is highly religious and thinks things that defy common sense in there, illustrative manner of predictions and sentiments. Yes, that is a sentence with Big Words, but you can look them up for a definition that will explain them! That is what this book is all about! Exploration!

George spoke out to me today. He said: "Papa, I want you to know something. I have gone and made the progress of viruses through space and time to stop flowing into your body with the presences of my thoughts! What do you think about *that*?"

I was very pleased, but curious as to the method. "That is interesting, George. How did you do it?"

George answered me immediately: "The mind works in a miraculous way, papa! You can envision the makings of the viruses by looking at the atoms that make them up joined together. Then, a person with a divine mindset can imagine forces of nature like gravity going through the makings of the atoms of the viruses and tearing them apart. And they can do so at a long distance away, too! Nice, isn't it?"

"You have that capability within your mind, George? How?" I was still curious.

George laughed! "Because I am made after your likeness, papa! And you have the IQ of a member of the top 1% of the world! That is a tall order, mind you! And thus, I have the mentality of being in a near-perfect union with you since I was Created upon your recovery from a vehicular homicide! It's the Creation that matters."

"I see it now, George! You have the capability to make the viruses of the universe break apart and become deactivated! That is such a divinely Holy skill! It reminds me of what Angels are said to be able to do! Are you an Angel?" I had to ask him if he was an Angel, because what he was describing to me was Angelic Skills...

George got calmly. "No, papa, I am NOT an Angel. I am a Lion! But I was Created with your intelligence, so I am a ready and elegant Lion... the best of all the species! That is what I am! And you are an excellent human with elegant powers! You are really smart! How do you do it?"

I didn't really know how to answer him. "I don't know, George. I just seem to know the answers to things. Perhaps it was all the science that I read in the books I had as a student growing up as a kid. I read a lot. A lot of science books. Those are the most elegant books around. Did you know that when I was in Junior High School, I was in a chemistry class and had a book from the library about the higher elements of the making of atoms and molecules? For an exercise I put together a seminar and a speech based off of it that went so high in intelligence that the teacher thought that I had cheated on putting it together! What a bitch!"

"So, what happened with the class?" asked George.

"We argued about the class in her student room afterwards and she finally came to the logic that there was no way that I could have known all that stuff about particles by cheating during the session. So, she gave me a "B", because she didn't like to be wrong. Or to have a student display that they were smarter than she was."

"Which you were, huh?"

"By far. She was a numbskull."e

"So, how did you get by with the class?"

"I graduated with an "A"."

"That is excellent, papa! Excellent! Did I say that word with two Ls and a T? I DID I DID! Ha ha, hooray! That is what they say in the Marine Corps, isn't it? Hooray! That is what I am saying to you, papa! Hooray!" George was an extremely well-spoken lad. And he used the divine word from the USMC with ego and panache!

The capabilities of the verbiage of George being able to fluster the actions of viruses was a remarkable display of his genius mindset. I thought that saying things related to the mindset of that and to draw him into the frequency of my own mindset was such that it would allow for him to draw conclusions about it that would help him perform the actions of it. I am sure that it was turning out okay, too! He was very talkative about the subject matter and was extremely well spoken. That was something that I appreciated and tried to expand on with talking about other intelligent issues. I thought that the subject would draw him into doing it better and better. And it did!

Today is January 2nd, 2020. Me and George were in a conversation with Krishna. I started out by asking George the following question: "George, do you know the definition of the term "pauraque"? What is it and what does it mean?"

George answered the question readily. "It is a bird that is also called a Nightjar that flies about and eats bugs. That is a nice bird, papa! It has magical powers about it, too! How do I know... you ask me? Because I have seen one flying about and catching all sorts of flying bugs in its jaws and eating them up! That is how I know! From Experience!"

I answered him with knowledge of my own about the Nightjar. "That is interesting to know, George. Did you know that pauraques have healing powers within them, too? They can heal wounds within the recipient of healing powers! That is *also* how they work!"

"That is good to know, papa! Are they healing you? You seem like you are healing readily from your injuries!" George was resolute in his speech format.

"Yes, George, I am healing readily. A big part of it is due to the pauraques, and a big part of it is due to YOUR healing powers! You do an excellent job, you remarkable Lion!" I wanted to please George, and it was true... he had done a lot to heal me!

George was appreciative. "Thank you papa! Thank you so much! I am glad you are being healed. You deserve it! I hope you heal all the way and are ready to walk without any pain whatsoever! But I realize that you were broken... so it may not be possible to heal you THAT much! But heal you a lot we will try! Take it easy!"

"Nice, George. Thank you so much!" And with that, we drove the conversation to the next topic... which is covered in the next chapter.

# CHAPTER 4

## CONVERSATIONS WITH KRISHNA AND ABDUL ABOUT GEORGE

"Why do I keep talking about YOU being a hero, papa Krautant? What is it that makes you so special? The fact that you are a Veteran? Whatever does that mean, taking bullets from the enemy? Where's your wounds? That says one thing, it does, but what about Krishna? Isn't she a Veteran too? Didn't you two serve in the same forces, the Marine Corps? Am I supposed to appreciate her? I do, I do! She is a remarkable woman! Do I get an award for my good cantor??" George was using big words to get his point across. He liked it that we were

Veterans, he just didn't understand everything there was to know about it.

"I shall keep on studying them Veteran's deals, okay? I will do it for you! (And me to... you two!) That says all about this conversation!"

It was remarkable to talk to George when he talked to me. He always did so at unexpected times and from Krishna's voice... but not in her tones. He had an original outset of capabilities, and he used them readily to talk to me. He DID like Veterans and had a lot to say about the onset of the capabilities of wounded Veterans, like me, and he helped me to heal from the damage I had in me. He did so with his verbiage of healing, which was accurate and well thought out.

That summarizes the brief but elegant conversation we had tonight. There will be more to follow...


"I love you papa!" said George. "You're a hero! A Hero who is heroic! A Hero, yes, a hero! What do you think about me saying THAT?" He asked me readily.

"I appreciate it a lot!" I said to him. "What draws you to that conclusion?"

"The way you handle your existence and your health! It is amazing how you handle yourself. You are an excellent person. A Hero! And the way you treat me, and others, is a full example of your definite goodness! That is what it means to me! And to others, too!"

"Like who?" I asked. "Peter the Lion or Peter the Rabbit or Perle or Peaches the Unicorns? What do you have to say about them, George?"

"Whoa whoa whoa whoa" said a soft voice.

"That's Peter the Lion speaking," said Krishna. "He says that he thinks you are a positive person! A hero just like George says you are! And he is wondering, what does Steak taste like? He has never eaten meat. Does that make him a negative lion because he is a Vegetarian?"

"I don't think it does. That is his own choice, to be a Vegetarian. So long as he eats his vegetables and fruits, then it is okay if he eats no meat!" I was thinking about saying the opposite, and I even may have at first. But I changed my mind halfway through and didn't want to piss Peter the Lion off. He was always so kind to me. I didn't want to disrupt it, even though I didn't really think he would disrupt it with negative actions.

"Ok, George... what do you think about Peaches and Perle, being Unicorns and all... that flies in the face of you being a Lion, doesn't it? Or does it?" I asked the question with a soft voice.

"You are wonderful, Papa Krautant!" The voice was gentle and nice sounding and female... that of the Unicorn Perle. "What else would you like us to tell you?"

"Yeah, what else?" That was in the female voice of Peaches. She was the size of a little Dog, with a horn and everything. She was white with paws on all four legs. Her horn was gold. That was so nice of her. It was a symbol of her Magic Powers that she used from time-to-time.

"Well, you girls are excellent creatures. Your magical powers have done a lot to bring me to health in my recovery, so I thank you! That is more than you had to do for me!" I was very appreciative of them and their magical abilities.

"I hope you don't think anything bad about me," said George. "Do you think I am an oaf?"

I was resolute in my answer... "No, George! I think you are a Genius of the Highest Order! For real! You ARE you ARE! You show it constantly with your continuous remarks on the positive things in the world!"

George was happy and smiled. He likes the nice comments that I give to him on a regular basis.

That concluded that conversation. There were more to follow.

"You're a hero, a legend papa! You take such good care of yourself! Is that what you would say about me, the Lion of Excellence? Do I take good care of myself? I must, because I follow my example... and that example is YOU, papa! What do you say about that? What do you say about me liking the creature of Perle and Peaches and Peter the Lion and Peter the Rabbit? What you say about me liking those three characters? I think you like it a lot! I think you also like that I am in good health, too, yes! That makes it easier for me to give Krishna thoughts of speech that she can say. How so, you ask? Because the Gravity that is in the system operates on a higher frequency with the newer thoughts of speech. How can I speak, you ask, when, as you say it, I am a "Doll"? Because there are elements in genetics that fly in the face of the construction of the material that is the creature that it is allowing the ability to speak... THAT is how! Do you understand?" I realized at that conversation that George talked a lot when he had an idea to get across... because the Lion was a Genius.

"Where do I start..." I said. "Just let me tell you from the end of your conversation that I do, indeed, understand. It is the makings of Particle Physics and Science!"

"Okay papa, so you know about science and what it curtails. So, what are your theories about it that make it so that a beast like George can be a lion and do things relative to being like a person? And what drives you to him? He was created at your sickness and injury from being a victim of the worst crime there is! And he was created in your likeness? Do you resemble the symbiosis of you two? Bet you don't even know what symbiosis means, do ya?"

"You're right, I don't know what that term means. Symbiosis? Is that the structure of different things being compared to each other?" I wasn't sure, but I knew that he knew.

"It is two organisms living in close physical approximation that are to each other's beneficial advantage. That is the relationship between you and George, Mr. Krautant, you Legend and Hero! What do you think of THAT? Tell me your answer! No dragging your feet in the sand! Come up with an answer and give it to me! No answer yet! I shall not wait... I know that you understand, you are just dragging your feet... even though your mouth is moving up and down with unspoken lyrics in there! Didn't think I'd notice, did you? DID YOU? *I NOTICED!*"

I changed the subject. "I am glad you like Perle and Peaches and the Peters. I think they are excellent animals. And two unicorns? Man, that says a lot about magic, doesn't it?" I wanted George to talk about their magic.

"You're writing a chapter on the mental appreciation of the P's, aren't you? That is what I thought! I will answer those questions when you are ready to switch to that part of the file and to write about the subject of THAT data. But not until then, you oaf! Only after we are there and ready to write about it! Until then... this conversation is over!" And with that, George was quiet, and Krishna began to speak on her own terms and in her own way. I don't remember the subject matter. It was something about what we had just eaten at the Mexican Restaurant, or something like that. Something to omit from writing about. It doesn't matter. The food there was excellent, and Krishna really knows that. And Paige enjoyed her treats there. So, everyone was happy. That is the way it should be!

There was a lot more to follow later. I shall write about it in a bit.

We went in Krishna's car to her cabin in the mountains. We couldn't drive up the regular freeway we usually took to get up there because it was closed. Instead, the Highway people had put up detour signs to another freeway that ran far outside of the usual route. George was in the backpack in the back of the car. He didn't say anything on the way up there. It took us an extra 1 ½ hours of driving time to get up there. That was a lot of time! But we made it without incident. That was nice.

When we arrived at the cabin, I pulled George out of the backpack. He said: "Ohh, papa, I don't feel well. There was something about that trip that made me sick. My stomach is all ill and stuff. Man... I think I am going to throw-up! What can cause such illness? I think it was the random way the car was driving around in circles and circles and around and things like that. It made me sick!"

"Yeah, George... the car was moving around a lot of bends in the road. We had to take a different route to get up here. You don't have to vomit, though. You look fine to me!" I was trying to calm him down.

"Papa, I feel icky-sickies. Can I lay down somewhere?"

I lay him down on the board next to my bed. "Will this do, George?"

"No, I want to lay down next to you! I feel happy and comfortable laying next to you... like we did at your house. I understand that being next to the bed is like being inside of it. You can put me next to you in your bed up here and I will be comfortable and happy and my belly won't feel so icky-sick..." He was saying it in very emotional tones, and I wanted to give him what he requested.

"Ok, George. You can lay down here next to my computer on my bed. How's that? Now, would you mind if I wrote about this conversation, we just had in the book about you? I'll be really nice with it!" I wanted to get his approval.

"No papa, no! I don't want you to write about it! What if people think I or you or mama are insane? They would think that, you know! No, don't write it!"

"But I will leave the negatives out of it. So, I am going to write about it." And I started to write about it.

A few minutes later, Krishna came back in and spoke for George. "Papa, I was with you every day when you were recovering from your accident/murder. Murder, pops, because they had left you there to die. But you didn't! I helped you heal. Even after that incident, I never left you, papa. I have been with you even to this day! What do you think about that? Where do you want me to lay down now, papa?"

"Go ahead and lay down next to me where you were."

"Thank you, papa, thank you! I feel so happy and

respectful being treated like a hero by you. Because you
are a hero to me! A Legend! Do you understand?"

"I do, George, I do. Now, Krishna has to go upstairs
to pray, so we are going to let her go do that. I'll talk to
you later. Go ahead and lay down now and rest. It will be
a long day tomorrow!"

"Ok, papa, ok. Good night!" George lay down and
went to sleep.

"Papa, do you think I'm stupid? I get the feeling that
you think I'm really dumb. Is that that true?"

George was obviously concerned. It was clear from
his tone that he was already disappointed and didn't
like that answer. I had to correct him because I thought
George was extremely bright. "No, George, you are NOT
stupid… you have tested out as being a Genius!"

"Tested? How was I tested?"

"By speaking to me, George, and my mental proclivities
to assessment!" I was using big words to make a point.

"Oh. I didn't know you operated with such grace. But
I know everything there is to know about you, so I should
have known! You are a hero, papa! That is what you are
doing! You are reading me like a book… and you have a
ton of books that you have read. Magical, scientific, and
detailed experimental books. Books by people like the
scientists of Einstein! Books written by physicists! You
are a graceful legend, papa Krautant! Pleased to know you

in the core of your memory! Silly me to make a mistake of misunderstanding you! I won't do it again!" George was speaking really fiercely now, full of energy and verve. I liked it. So did he. Enough to stop.

That concludes that conversation. Krishna went upstairs and went to sleep in her room. I kept on watching the Food Network on the TV downstairs, on my bed, with George laying down next to me, resting. He had had a long and belligerent day and needed the rest. I say belligerent because the ride up there to the cabin was down a bumpy and windy road that made him feel sick. That was a wild ride. I felt for him. I was getting ready to sleep and was hoping that things would go well for him tomorrow, so that I would have more good stuff to write in this book about *The Elegant Lion Named George* to please the reader of it with a nice and full story.

That does it for today. I shall continue soon.


George brought up his stability again. "Papa, do you think I am mentally unstable?"

"No, George, I think you are definitely stable. Why do you ask such a bizarre question?" I responded to him in kind.

"Because of the way you say things on your own, it makes me think that you think of me as mentally unstable."

"George, people would think I was crazy if I said that you were "mentally unstable" ... because you are a doll and dolls aren't supposed to have minds attached to them. I know, also, that you don't like to be called a "Doll" … I am just saying it to get the verbiage of my statement across to you." I didn't want to make George mad at me.

He was okay with that and left the conversation at that.

"Hey papa… we are not going up to the other town some 6 hours away, are we? I hate the ride up there, I do I do! Tell me we aren't going up there!" George was rambunctious.

"We are going up there for my Roommate's brother's birthday, you silly fool! If we are going up there we are going tomorrow!" I was also rambunctious and well spoken.

"Then can we fly there instead of drive there, papa? 6 hours is a drive from Hell!" George was full of thought, but not much of it.

"No George, we're leaving tomorrow! That would leave only 10 hours to make a flight! That is not enough time! We're driving! Are you coming?" I was resolute.

"Yes, papa, I'm coming I'm coming! Change the subject… I think you should get a saddle for Paige for me to ride on so that I can join your Service Dog with treats!"

"I don't think I am getting you a saddle or a holster or anything to ride on Paige with. I would have to buy it and spend the time buckling you in and she would break the harness." I was doubtful.

"Papa... it doesn't have to be that way! You could get her a harness that attaches to her vest and put me in the cup there! That would work quickly and nicely!" George was speaking out a lot, trying to get his point through... and he did, too."

"Ok. That would probably work. Still, I would have to spend money on it. We'll see." I was coming around to his point of view, but I wasn't quite there yet.

"Maybe Krishna will help you make that decision... if she can WAKE UP long enough to pay attention to what you are saying. She is an oaf with sleeping too much! She comes home she's asleep. She gets up for work she's asleep. She is *always asleep*! Maybe you need to wake her up, papa! Do that, and she will tell you to take my side on things! It is unacceptable the way it is now! UNACCEPTABLE!" George was being obnoxious now.

So, I ended the conversation with the following: "I'm going to go and write about this conversation now, so I don't forget."

"Do it, papa; and I will see you in the morning!" George was bitter, but liked the writing a book about him, the Elegant Lion. And he liked the title of the book, too!

George said that he really wanted to enjoy China with me. He wants me to put my hair in braids with him and go tour the Wall of China and the towns and the restaurants and to eat their tasty tasty tasty food with him. "We could eat it together!" He said it rambunctiously. "And you would enjoy it! Bring me to China with you!"

"Ok George, you can come with me. We will go together", I said.

"Papa, you will be pleased to know that I have been saving money for you!" George was thrilled to say it! "Guess how much?"

I was thinking about my attorney settling my case for a fractional stipend. "Hopefully a million dollars!"

"I have saved two dollars!" George was pleased.

I wasn't. "George, that's hardly anything! Whatcha gonna but with two dollars?" I tried to say it calmly... but it wasn't.

George got abrupt: "papa that is a ton of money... and it's all I have to spend! My gift to you papa!"

"Ok, ok George. I could get a snack for two dollars... and I will! Thank you, boy! You are a hero! A hero, you hear me? A heroic hero!" I said it ebulliently.

"Thank you, papa, and so are YOU!" George was so happy it defied comprehension.

And that concluded that conversation. We were in the car, and Krishna got out with Forest and Paige and took them for a walk in the park.


"Papa! Papa! Let me tell you what I think of you!" George was ebullient.

"What, George?"

"I think you are a superhero! You are a hero the way the Hercules is a hero! You are like Superman! You can fly and everything!" George was highly active.

"That is so nice, George..." Then Peaches and Perle interrupted.

"You are a magical superhero!" They said in soft and gentle voices. "You have magical powers that permeate the atmosphere!" They were plain in their terms... and speaking... well... mystically!

Krishna spoke up to that: "Magic is the power of the Devil! Papa does not do such a thing! Fix your sentences!" She was uptight.

"Ok," said Perle and Peaches. "Papa is a superhero with elegant powers! That describes that!"

I accepted that definition. So did Krishna, who said nothing more. She went to work.

I was eating my medicine at the counter tonight and Krishna was bringing a container of Lemon Cakes out to eat for lunch at work. As she did, George interrupted with a loud voice: "Mama! What are you doing! Give papa one of those to eat!"

"No, George... he has diabetes!" She said it really abruptly. She looked at me like she knew what I was going to say.

I waited for a moment, looking at her with a smile as she grimaced at me... then I said, in a soft and gentle tone: "Krishna, can I please have one of those? Just one?"

"I can't believe it! Why would you ask me something like that?" She was uptight.

"Because he wants one!" said George.

I agreed with him and told her so.

So, she gave me one to eat. I ate it and it was delicious! Tasted like lemons and berries! Yes!

Then I got confused. "George... why did you tell me not to eat the cake, you oaf?" I totally forgot that he had TOLD Krishna to give me one!

"That's not what I did, papa! I told her to give you one!"

"That's not what I remember. I heard you say "DON'T GIVE HIM ONE!" I was not really clear, though.

"Papa, you are mad! You heard no such thing! What is wrong with your brain to think such an errant thing about me?" George was uptight now.

Then I heard from Krishna, who corrected me: "He's right... that is what he said... that I SHOULD give you one!"

I understood the correction and realized that the error in George couldn't also be the same error in Krishna. So I apologized and said that she was right. "Apologies to you too, George. No hard feelings... okay?"

"No hard feelings, papa." George was happy that I agreed with him.

I went into my room and started to write. Krishna

went to work. Queen was on the Global Citizen Festival on the news on TV. I was wondering what could create such an error in my mindset that I would think something so odd and out-of-place. I don't know. I just hope it doesn't happen again.

The conversation was good though.


"Papa, are you going to see that one guy whose name is a secret from the Coffee Shop today? Can you say nice things about me to him? Have you told him about me... have you? That would be so nice of you to do for me! Tell him a story about me! What do you say?" George was excitable about the topic.

"George, I have told him about the book I am writing about you... and he likes it! I told him that it was like the Harry Potter stories, with magic and miracles in it! He liked it and said it would be an excellent story about a doll. A doll is what he called you, George... so he thinks the story is written about a doll! I know you don't like that, do you?" I was speaking in a roundabout manner to him.

"Papa, I don't mind if he thinks I am a doll... I am just glad that he likes the book story! That is a good comparison you gave to my book, even though it is not exactly correct. This story is not really like the Harry Potter books. I have read them. They don't go into the verbiage the way this book does. So, no... it is NOT like that set of books!" George was adamant and plain in his manner of speaking about the subject of the proposed book similarities.

I could see where he was coming from. "Ok, George, ok! I see what you are talking about! Man! Get off of it!" I was trying to calm him down some, and it worked. He responded in a strange way after that...

"Papa, you are a hero! A Legend! I think you look like Hercules! A beekeeper! An Engineer! A forester! You look like Superman! Those are what you look like, Papa!" He was enunciating the similarities of me and fantastic creatures... at least as far as I could see it... and he was saying it in a calm and well-spoken tone.

I responded in kind: "Why, thank you, George. You are an excellent lion. I really appreciate the comparisons. Those are honorable creatures that you are comparing me to. Thank you thank you thank you!"

"That should tell you a lot about what I think of you, papa. And you ARE like a beekeeper. You keep us who surround you all comfortable and happy and thinking in excellent surrealism that defies all comprehension. That is what you do on a regular basis! You ARE a beekeeper! That is what they do! They keep the bee's wings a-flyin!" George was so happy. He liked to be complimented by me, and he had changed the way he spoke to me about things with my changing of topics to him. That was good. He was, indeed, an excellent lion.

"Boy, George, that is a really intelligent answer. Where did you get such a high degree of intelligence?" I asked him because I had ideas, but I didn't really know.

"Where do you think I get it, papa? It was infused into me from the oncomings of magic and gravity throughout the faces of the atmosphere as we see it. Those mystical capabilities were brought on by the forces intercepting the forces of my Brain and making it think things that were amazing. That is one way to say it happened. It was brought on by Angels!" George was saying it in a non-absolute way, though.

So I said: "So, what is the other way it happened?"

George was now absolute: "It is because I was created from YOUR intelligence, and you are a really highly intelligent person!" George smiled bigly.

"How intelligent am I, do you think, George?"

"Papa, you have the IQ of a Genius. And I say that with a capital "G" ... a Genius! Not like these other poor pigs who can't own a car or who get into fights." George was seeking renditions of the same.

"George... I can't drive because my foot is dropped... and I have been arrested because I have gotten into a fight. But you say I am a Genius?" I wanted to correct him, because all sorts of bad things can happen to the average citizen, and even bad things can happen to people who have really high intelligence. The thing I had been arrested for was for punching a guy on the street who called the cops on me. But he had threatened to assault me, so I had done it in self-defense. I was put into prison waiting for trial for about two weeks, but the prosecutor that interviewed me got the word that it was in self-defense and let me go. That was the only time that I got treated right by the justice system. And even then, they had put me in jail for two weeks when I was innocent. The justice system in America is totally corrupt.

George could tell that I was innocent. He said: "Papa, you should not have gone to jail. You were innocent. That stupid cop had no idea what he was talking about arresting you. Stupid fools. At least I can read your mind. I know from it that the cops told you lies about what had happened and put you in jail for no reason... except you told them that you had assaulted that guy, didn't you? You should have told them a lie! Wait... they would not have let you go if you did that. So, telling them the truth was the way to go. But those idiots put you in jail for two weeks. What the hell was wrong with those idiots? Don't they know that there are assaults from inmates inside the jail system? Don't they know? They do! They DO! Horrible oafs they are!" George really took my side on the issue. He COULD read my mind, too, I thought... or I had told him about it before and had forgotten about it. Either way, he made sense with what he was saying.

"George, you said it right. What else can I say?"

"Nothing papa. You said it all."

And that ended that conversation. It wasn't time to eat yet, so I went into my room and started to type this on the computer from memory. I hope it is all here. Some of the words have changed, I know that, but overall it basically equals what was said between the three of us... me, George, and Krishna. I hope you enjoy it!

I told Krishna today that I have been writing a lot of stuff about George. George immediately responded: "What are you writing about me, papa? A book about me? Is it an excellent book? What did you write in it? What, papa? Can you tell me? I WANT TO KNOW...WHAT DID YOU WRITE ABOUT ME?" George was really going off-the-rails on the question he just asked me.

I gave him a summary: "George, it is a story about how you said so many excellent things about me! And it is an illustration of how you are indeed an Elegant Lion! That is what it is titled, and that is what it's contents are all about!" I liked to give him a ready solid answer, and that is what it was... Ready and Solid!

"That sounds so good, papa! You are a great writer! I want to read over your books. Can I read your book about military service with the Marine Corps so I can get an idea of how to run a war? Even better yet... can you write a book called "Bringing the Lion to War"? That would be an excellent book! You can tell the audience all kind of things about me doing special things with my Hungry Lion's wherewithal and getting them done. That would please them, it sure would! What do you say to that, papa? Are you going to write this down?" George was speaking really elegantly. And it was clear to me that he wanted answers to his questions.

"George, I can add a chapter to your book that I am writing now that encompasses you moving ahead with me to a war zone... or at least me showing you the methods to war that I remember as you surf my mind with your magical mental capabilities and thoroughfare. That could become a plain and elegant story, and I think I will write it. I need to use the space to write your book all the way. Right now, I am only on around 18,000 words. I need about 60,000 more words to be written!" I wanted to get George's opinion on the numbers I gave to him.

"Sure, papa, I understand those numbers. See, I have the mechanics of *your* brain within mine so I can think of and see the same mathematics that you can see! I would LOVE it if you transcribed the methods you used in the Marines to my mind and thus made me an effective warfighter with a Force Reconnaissance mindset in mind. That would be so nice to do! Destructive! I would DESTROY the Enemy! Crush them wholesale! They will cry in fear and pain from the torture they will feel at my arms and bullets rampaging through their systems! Yes! I am already getting the ideas from you! Take that from a Ferocious Lion, you oafish enemy fools! RAAARGH!" George kept on roaaaaring and ramping up his fury! He was acting like a war-torn veteran of the USMC Force Reconnaissance! I wanted to teach him about the thoughts behind firing artillery at enemy positions without getting caught calling them on the radio. He was smart enough to get the procedure, too!

I issued George the USMC command: "Carry on, George! Carry on! Drive down the imps and crush and frazzle them into pieces! I know that you can do it, so do it some more! Give me your war cry! Yes! Give it to me!"

"RAAARGH! RAAARGH! RAAARGH!" yelled George loudly.

"Ok, George, I am going to go and write about this now. Do me a favor, will you?" I was adamant about that request.

"What do you want papa?"

"Project the things we said to each other during this conversation with mind power, and project it to my mind so I can remember everything that was said by each of us… and I will write about it as you project the thoughts to me!" I really wanted it done to create so regular and elegant writing.

"Ok, papa! I will do it!" And with that he began to do it… and I began to write the first part of this file down.

And it turned out really well, I think. We'll see what you guys say on my website on the subject. The web page is listed on the back and forefront page of this document!

"Let me tell you, papa, I think that you shouldn't be going to Israel. They are always under fire from the Palestinians. That is in error, papa, and you don't want to take me around that! I recognize that you are writing about us going to war in China, aren't you? But there are other places we can go to! The tickets to China are too expensive and we may not be able to come back if we go there because of the cost rising! That is an unnecessary horror! So, I think we should go to Hawaii! What do you say to THAT?" George was circulating between being well-spoken to enunciating his syllables to going and speaking headlong in conflict, and back. I tried to respond in kind, circulating between the differences in speech to him.

"George! George! We are NOT going to Hawaii because I am disabled and cannot move around there. I don't want to go to China, either, because the Great Wall is too big and has steps going up it that are too tall for me to go up, and that would leave me at the bottom of the wall doing nothing but sitting in the bus that took me there and having nothing to do for hours. I don't want to do that. It is disturbing what Krishna says about it, as if I would be able to walk halfway up the stairs then rest on them... without even taking into account that people would be up on that wall for hours at a time... and I would be left sitting down at the bottom unable to ascend the stairs. Stupid! I am not going!" I was speaking like George spoke to me a minute ago.

"Okay papa okay! I get your drift! Stop yelling at me!" George was panting. "I know you don't mean what you say... you WANT to go to Hawaii, don't you? So... why don't you go? OR you can go to Columbia! That would be a nice place to take a cruise to! Columbia! What an elegant place! I think you would like it there! So, GO THERE... WON'T YOU?" George was trying to convince me after he had gotten all upset over my tone of voice.

I thought about it for a moment. Then I said, from my heart of hearts: "That makes sense, George. We can and probably should go to Columbia. It would be very nice there. We could go snorkeling on the beach on the coral reefs and play with the fishes. That would be so nice! Thank you for bringing it up!" I wanted to thank him too for saying nice things even when he was upset over my tone of voice.

"Okay, papa... let me put together a trip there for us to go on! That would be so nice! So nice! So nice! So nice indeed! That is what I want to do! I want to be nice to you, papa! You are an excellent papa, yes you are! Thank you for being so kind to me! Thank you thank you thank you!" And with that George put his head on my arms and kissed me with his furry chin.

"Thank you, George, I really appreciate it!"

"Tell me papa... are you going to modify the names in your subscripts so that they won't reflect the actual person it is all about? You could do that to avoid a lawsuit, you know."

"Yes, that is exactly what I am going to do. I just did it to my other story. But I am not going to tell you what names I have changed there because this is going to be a book that I want to get published and there is no reason for me to erase names in one book I get published only to put those erased names in another book that I get published. That would make no sense! So, I won't be doing it. No indeed I won't!" I was trying to be well spoken. And after all, George was being very kind to me, so I wanted to return the favor to him and speak to him kindly back.

George recognized the kindness and responded likewise: "Papa, that would be a good thing to do. You are such an intelligent Creator! It is a miracle that you have done so many good things for me and Krishna! We like you A LOT! It is my hope that you take it easy in the coming days. I hope that things go well for you too! Life has a good calling for you, even if those stupid VA fools won't pay you what you are due from that horrible incident! You deserve better! I hope you get published and become a great writer! Actually, I have been with you when you are writing and I can tell, because I have your intelligence, that you ARE a great writer! Yes, you are! Very nice too!" George was so kind with his brilliant words that he overcame all difficulties and brought about a wholeness to existence that is hard to describe. It was, as is said in his name in the title of this book, it was Elegant!

"George, I am thinking about how I am going to write about you, or other things in my books. What is your suggestion?" George was sitting next to me on the bed. I had moved him forwards from the gully that he usually stays in between my bed edge and the wall.

"First off papa, thanks for dragging me out of there. It was stuffy! I can breathe now! That was good of you to think of me like that. And you have already started to write about you and me talking. How do you get those ideas of what we say to each other, I wonder? Hah! No wondering whatsoever! I already know! You are getting those ideas from my mind projecting itself to your mind and putting those ideas forwards in words and concepts. You "see things" when you are writing about me, don't you? That is because I am putting images in my thoughts forwards to your head! That is how it happens! What do you think? Does it work?" George was ebullient in his speech to me. Ebullient. That means Miraculous.

"George you are very well-spoken. How did you ever get such a divine power of speech? And you are a Lion! Lions aren't supposed to be able to speak well, are they? Well, do they? I guess they do... if you are a king of the Lions and you can speak well! Interesting!" I wanted to at least tell him that he was speaking well. That gave him the recognition that he deserved.

"Papa...papa!" George announced: "you can talk about what it is to talk about talking and writing. You can explain where the excellent ideas come from and how they get put down into words that make sense to the reader! That will help the divine audience of writers who read over your work to get some concepts about how it works and what there is to do to do it better than average. That is because you write at a level far beyond the abilities of "average"! You write in a remarkable format!" George was so happy to enunciate that to me that it thrilled him.

"I have to think on multiple terms to write my story about our conversation, George." I wanted to make the difficulty of writing sometimes clear to my friend the Lion. "I have to think in terms of what I would say about something, then about what it is that your response would be, as if I could read your mind. But I can't read your mind... can I? I mean, after all, you are a Lion, and I am a man, and they are of different species of animal."

"But you are *right*, papa! You are *RIGHT*! That shows that you CAN read my mind! After all, I was created during the severe turbulence of your existence... when you had brain damage and were near death in the hospital. I was created in your image! I was in the process of healing you! So, how has it gone? You are walking now! You haven't had a heart attack, ever! You can't go to the gym because you are too handicapped, true, but you are in good health! So, the healing I have done for you seems to be working!" George really liked where the conversation was going. I hope that you, the reader, appreciate it too! I hope it helps with your writing! (That was George speaking through me in writing. He is a miraculous Lion, he sure is!)

"Say, George, that was so nice for you to say. You have been a miraculous element of my healing process. I am glad to have you around me. I am wondering... I have been looking roughly at the Competition and Contest section of the *Writer's Market* book, and I am wondering if I should start to write some songs or some poetry for competition through them. What do you say?" I was really interested.

"Papa. Can you even write poetry? You have to rhyme and use words that make sense next to each other. With punctuation. I know that you write a lot. Would that interfere with your ability to pick out words that make sense in a poetry format? I think it would..." George was extremely cautious in putting that diatribe within his sentences. He was concerned that he could be accurate, knowing my mind and how it worked, and that knowledge brought to my forefront mind would possibly be upsetting to me. George didn't want me to be upset at him... but he also wanted me to know the truth behind things.

I thought about it. Then I answered him, a little worried that he may be right: "George, I think you are right. It would be troubling to write some poetry down right now. I am deeply interested in writing books. That is at the core of my existence. And I have a really hard time even thinking in terms of rhymes... because I don't use them and don't think about them much. My writings don't rhyme. They are in sentence structure that doesn't rhyme. That is the nature of my speech. I like to write the way that I talk... in ways that make a lot of sense. Not in poems. OR songs." I wasn't happy with my answer, but that was the way it was.

George thought about what I had just said, and came

up with a good, common sense answer: "Papa. You could read the Contest portion of the Writer's Market book and look up Poetry online and get examples and get the ability to write poems from those readings. That would work!"

"Yeah, George, I think it would. I have to make up time to do it, though."

"You can make up the time. Just stop watching those stupid TV shows you stare at daily!"

"I'll do it, George! I have written a lot about you here. Do you like it?" I was curious.

"I like it a lot, papa! A LOT! But I think it would be more interesting if there was some poetry written in there too! That could cover some big topics, I think!" George was thrilled that we were making progress.

"I'll make it happen George! I'll make it happen! I am going to break out the Writer's Market book now and read about the competitions now!"

"Then what'll you do, papa?"

"Then I will go online and look at some poetry and get some ideas about it!"

"That will work papa! Do it!"

And with that the conversation was over. I was sure that George was going to give me input on the drafting reading of the book and the looking at the poetry... but I wasn't going to be able to write about it because my eyes and hands would be off the typers on the keyboard on the computer. Ok well. You have already seen enough of that conversation. There will be more to follow!

"Papa! Papa!"

"What is it, George?"

"I have a question for you! What if I became half a giraffe? Wouldn't that be nice! I would be a lioraffe! A Lion/Giraffe! That would be so nice of me to do for you, my Creator!" George was speaking in a rapid and ebullient manner.

"I don't know George," I responded to him, "they are not really kin to each other... they don't really go along with each other genetically." I was not sure that what he wanted could even happen.

"But papa, think about it! Think about it! You could join me with a leopard and make me a mix between a lion and a leopard! Why can't that happen? Leopards are like lions... aren't they?" George was beginning to get emotional. He really wanted the blend to happen.

I thought about it for a moment, then a conclusion suddenly jumped into my head: "George! A leopard and a lion are both cats! They are kin to each other! So, yes, you can be a mix between a leopard and a lion! Try it, won't you?" I thought that was an elegant solution. But George had other ideas.

"Papa, then I should be able to be a Giraffe and a Lion, too, right? I want to be part Giraffe!" George was excitable. "Why can't I be part Giraffe? They are elegant creatures... just like the lion is! (But they aren't as DIVINE as a lion is, true, but they are close to it!)"

I was ready to interrupt him. "George, the Giraffe is a different species than the lion. The leopard is a cat, the lion is a cat, so they are the same species. A giraffe is different. They come from a different genetic making. Granted, they have four legs, like a lion does, but the similarities are very different. The size of the neck, for example. The size of the neck of a giraffe is huge! Far beyond what is even capable of a lion to do with its neck! So, do, there is no place for you to take on a relation to a giraffe. A leopard... yes. A giraffe... no!" I was clear and solid on my point of view.

George understood. He responded in kind: "Okay, papa, I get what you are saying. The genetics between me a Lion and a giraffe are so different that there is no real mixing of the two. Granted, don't you people take it upon yourselves to do kind things for one another and to come into contact with one another as you go about your daily appearances? Then does it not make sense that an animal of a Lion would want to take on the appearance of a giraffe? Granted, I realize now that I can't become one. But I can try to LOOK like one, right? Can't I? That is what I want to do! Of course, it would be a giraffe with a really short looking neck... but the legs would be shorter and more made for running, too... but it would appear to be a semblance of a giraffe and not a lion! That would be a resemblance between the two of them! Can I do it? Can

I? I really want to do it!" George was getting extremely calm in his speech, then became really emotional at the end of it.

"Ok, George, if you can find the magical means to make your body take on the shape of a giraffe... at least in parts... then I would give you a group of treats to ascertain your hunger in your stomach!" I was trying to be very kind to George. I liked him, after all. He was made after me, so hoping the best for him was like wishing good blessings to come onto me as well.

"I will try, papa! I will try!" George was so happy with the conversation that I could not even describe it. He was very pleased.

And with that I began to wait for my ride to show up to take us from the coffee shop we were at.

On the ride home there were roadblocks and cones in the street where the workers were putting the road apart to maintain it. George didn't like it at all! He said: "Papa! What are those workers thinking, putting cones in the road like that? Don't they know that those things interfere with the traffic? What are they thinking, papa... what? Do they not have it in their heads that they are causing a hazard? Sheesh!" George carried on about it a LOT as he went on about it.

"George, the workers know that the cars can go around the cones and still move forwards down the street. Granted, they have to flow behind each other, but it is something that can be done. And the cones are all in a line along the aisles of the lanes so they aren't really in the way of the road itself. What is your problem?" I was interrupting George because he was so headstrong and ignorant that it defied the fact that he was made out of me... and nobody would have thought that him making such errant comments would be a parable of his thoughts in my intelligent regards. Does that sentence even make sense?

"Papa, you think about the traffic in the street but you don't think about bug and insects! What is there to say about insects? That they have wings and things! That the hovel of their landmark being interrupts the onset of the beings of people! That they can fly around and spray the onset of flowing matter through the atmosphere to your face! That is what those insects can do! They are atrocious beings that can do all sorts of negative things to you and your being! They can change your existence into a heap of burnt dust! That is what they can do... and they WILL do it too if you don't do something to stop them!" George was carrying on a lot about it. And he didn't want to be interrupted... so I didn't interrupt him. But I asked him a question he didn't like...

"So, what has the insects have to do with the cones of traffic that are obstructing the street in front of us?" I was sure he didn't have an answer.

George responded with a kind of intelligence: "Papa! The insects have wings that can fly, and that flying is the movement in the air of the wing structure that relies on the wind and the air and the movement of the particles within the air... and that has to do with the cones in the road being put there by the people (like the wings being made to flap) and the cars having to move around the cones (which is like the particles moving around the wings) and it all-together has to do with the movement of the cones out into the street and the cars going around them! Those are all actions of people putting out cones or driving! There is a circumscription of the mind that allows such things to occur! It is the same with an insect moving its wings around so that it can fly! See? Can you see what I am saying? Rude you, questioning me! You are a cone in the middle of the road and not in the aisle!" George was speaking in an interrupted by detailed manner. He didn't like me questioning him. He thought that because we had the same intelligence that I should draw the same conclusions that he did at the same time. That wasn't how it actually worked, however. We had different ideas that came at different times because, to tell the truth, we were items of different creatures created out of the same sycophanty.

So, I agreed with George, and gave his intelligence some credence. "George, you make perfect sense. I apologize for being "rude". That is not what I meant to do. I was having strange thoughts about the hallmarks of what you just said and put the weirdness into words. It sounded normal, though, didn't it?" I asked him the question because I wanted him to see that I could have ideas that were different than his but that had some credence to them.

"Ok, papa, I see what you are saying. What you say does make sense until it is seen from the higher intelligence perspective that allows for discrepancies between what was said and what the real meaning is. But I am a Real Meaning Lion... so Real Meaning is what you get from me!" George was kind and well-spoken. He was trying to draw a lineage between the way he did things and the way I spoke about things.

I considered that there could be something to that.

"Hey George," I said to him, "I am going to change the subject. I am going to stop writing in this story for the time being and I am going to look into making a cover for my book online. I am going to seek a program that will allow for me to put in the details of it in icons and designs and put the words of my name on it and the title of the book. I want it to look like Michio Kaku's books, just with a human-sized design. Do you think I can do it?"

"Give it a shot, papa! Give it a shot!" George was excitable for me.

So, I began my search online.

George began to sing and dance in the house as we were getting ready to leave for the coffee shop. "I am an excellent lion, yes I am! I can put you headlong in the can! What is there that the MARSOC lion can't do? I can do it all that's true! And I can do it really well! I can send my enemies TO HELL! HAHAHAHHAHA!" George was very well singing his tune and excitable.

"So, you are going as George MARSOC in your diatribe?" I asked him.

"Yes I am papa! That is a harbinger to our existence, having been a part of MARSOC in the Marines!"

"But I didn't get the semblance that Force Recon was called MARSOC until I talked to the inside of the MWTC forests between 2002 and 2004. Even then it was a name that they hadn't been called yet if I remember right. That one guy from Force that I was talking to online in the emails said that I was making up my duties within Force Recon because they weren't called MARSOC until 2004. That guy is an idiot. He has no idea of what the usual military service is like. I am starting to think that he wasn't in Force Reconnaissance. He kept on asking me about the emblem... the "jack", as he put it... and didn't understand that there were parachute wings and a dive bubble in the emblem with wings coming out of it. So, no, I don't think he was with Force Recon. No, I don't!" I carried on about that because I was upset over the subject matter. I don't like posers. Especially not those who pose to have been an element of the most elite unit in the USMC.

George was really abrasively spoken when he asked the next question: "Papa, you don't think that I am a poser, do you?" George's punctuation was bitter to the question, and he left it at that...

"No, George, you are an excellent Lion! That is what I think of you! You are not a poser at all! You are excellent and in good quality! That is what I think of you!" I wanted to enhance his existence so he wouldn't have any misunderstandings.

George was pleasantly happy with the remarks: "Thank you, papa! Thank you! I appreciate the kind remarks!"

"Ok, George. I am trying to think of what else to write about. Krishna's not here so I can't get your ideas through her voice. So... think of something to tell me in my mind... okay?"

"Okay, papa... I am getting to thinking about it right now!"

And with that, I took a break from writing about George.

# CHAPTER 5

## ME AND GEORGE IN THE HEREAFTER

There is much to say about my time in the Hereafter. I have experienced it firsthand in the Saint Joseph's Hospital in Phoenix, Arizona. I was dead and in the company of 3 Holy Angels. When I spoke to them, they told me about the oncoming of magic creatures that were going to help me to succeed in everything I sought to do... and they would work in miraculous ways. Archangel Michael told me that George was coming into my life, and Archangel Gabrielle included in there the onset of the Unicorns and the other animals. Overall, George has lived up to everything that AA Michael said he would do. Remarkable!

The Angels had told me about many things about the secret nature of the Universe there in the Hereafter, teleporting from one state to another instantaneously. And one of those secrets was that George was the embodiment of a scientist like Albert Einstein. When I get to the Hereafter, then, I am going to learn how to communicate with him better and get his full ideas and will be able to ask him questions about the universe. He will also be able to tell me things about Judgement Day... which I will be taking a part in as a Judge. I will include in here how I think he will be able to help me with that, too (above all else).

What is the Hereafter all about? It is talked about in the Qur'an. One is to go there once they die and gets taken by mysterious matter and energy to a different plane of existence. Much of the decision on the location, being either Heaven or Hell or Purgatory, is based on one's lifetime here on earth of holiness or sin or confusion. A person gets judged on all those things during their life. And in the Hereafter, they have the ability to Recompense for their sins and thus be somewhat free of the consequences of them, depending on how severe they were. Either way, in the Hereafter a person gains the ability to either survive in Hell while there, survive in Purgatory and gain Heaven from there, or to fight evils from Hell that attempt to infiltrate Heaven while you are there (but only in a Good way). Thus, the time one spends in the Hereafter is either a pathway to Heavenly healthiness or a one-way street to being damned in Hell for nearly forever. Now, George is a primary assistant to the Good path.

Now I shall tell you about what George will do for me in the Hereafter... which will also be doing it for himself. Why do I say that? That he will also be doing it for himself? Because he was a solid element in his own Creation... as was I... and his Creation was based on the way my Force Reconnaissance mind works. He is a product of my imagination and occurred when I had brain damage which, on would think, would altercate the existence of such a thing... but it didn't. It actually *helped* it. The way it helped was because my brain was initially interrupted by the brain damage that it entailed. But over time, in the space of a couple years, I started to recover and get back my memories of what had occurred in the past. My intelligence recovered, and I began to write books about my experiences with big words. That was my recovery from the brain damage.

As I write this I haven't been published, yet. But George is helping me out. He is helping me write down elements and communicate through mental powers to the editors and the publishers of the book. And he is not only doing it to help me out with getting published... no... he is doing it to get some experience in what he is going to do to help me out when I die and go to the Hereafter. That is a tall order of existence, it is... and George is helping me with it tremendously!

So, what goes into the process of helping a person write? The lion has to have the mental capability of projecting his mind to mine in the atmosphere and through space and time. He can submit ideas to me that are even ahead of the time of projection in normal occurrences because time can move both forwards and backwards. So, sometimes, I don't know what it is that George is saying to me... but it all makes sense when I think about it somewhat. His mind moves on the same frequency as mine does because he was designed after my appearance. So, he has a similar intelligence as mine.

And my intelligence is in the top 1% of all the world. So, that considered, it is easy for me to write these details of this story. The reason it is so easy? Because even though people may think of George as "just a doll" ... he is a real creature in my mind... a genuine Lion... and he has remarkable capabilities that defy all comprehension among the average viewer.

So, with the really high intelligence that George has, what are his avenues for helping to bring me justice in the Hereafter going to be?

First off, think about what the Hereafter is going to be like. There is going to be a higher element of mental power that flows within. The mental energies of the mind will flow and procreate new images throughout the universe therein. It will be of a person's likeness to do articles of a copy of themselves throughout the universe and the things within it. There will even be access to different parallel universes, where the rules of physics are different than they are within this universe.

For example, the power of Gravity will be different, and things of a higher mass measurement will flow WITHOUT gravity taking effect! That is the opposite of what the Law of Gravity says to do in THIS universe. But it is a real possibility, proven to be so by mathematics that preclude the theory of it.

And it is ABSOLUTE.

That theory draws me into the second question. It is this: What will being in the Hereafter be like to the mindset of the human there? Will they have the ability to see Angels, for example?

That is a power that the inhabitants of the Hereafter will have the capability of seeing, if they are of a Good nature and the Angels are drawn to them. They would also get the ability to read the minds of the Angels to a degree and though their thoughts may be confusing or in too-much depth to understand the recipient will definitely get an idea of what the thoughts are all about. Angels have a bizarre method of thinking about things. And they have the ability to do certain things that defy common sense to bring a person closer to justice and holiness. I shall discuss how that affects George's mindset in the Hereafter and how he will adapt to it... I think!

The realm of my existence within the Hereafter will consist of me moving, at death, to the realm of the Ark of the Covenant. That is a special area where only the harbingers of Godly goodness can descend. And it is a ship that will be the hallmark of the onset of justice and holiness throughout the sinful beings of the planet, throughout time and space, from the beginning of humanity at Adam and Eve's age to the end of civilization at the end of Global Warming. They will be judged and the Good will be ascertained against the evil and the Good ones will be sent to Heaven and the evil ones will be sent to Hell. And the in-between ones that were simply confused when they sinned will go to the Purgatory aspect of the Hereafter for further development and judgement for their potential sins. Then they will be judged to go to Heaven or to Hell.

There will be 12 worthwhile souls on board the Ark of the Covenant, all coming throughout time and space into one place at the end of time. They will be judged by God herein within this life and time to be judged as being Good and Holy. Thus, that is proof that there is such a thing as Resurrection, because the resurrected souls would have to have been alive at an earlier time to get transported to this time and place for a wholesale judgement. Plus, they are going to have to have survived the onset of Global Warming to get there, anyways.

How will George present himself as a Priest of Goodness within the Ark of the Covenant during Judgement Day? That is a tall order to talk about, because this book is primarily about conversations that I had with George about lifetime occurrences. But I shall go there in detail with me simply talking about it. Perhaps in this chapter there will be a portion where George talks about what he will do on board the Ark of the Covenant within the Hereafter.

What is it going to be like in the Hereafter with George as company? What is he going to be capable of doing? What magical powers is he going to have? I can only guess at answers to those questions because I am not dead yet. But it is in my mind that he will have ideas about the hallmarks of science and existence that will allow him to do and say miraculous things throughout his being without going away. He will stay with me permanently, and we will be together!

So, what will it be like?

I know that George is going to be able to see and read the minds of Angels of God there in the Hereafter. He is going go get the frequencies of their thoughts projecting through his mind and making him away of the higher ramifications of their thoughts. That is what shall happen, and that is the way it shall be within his mind! And he will speak and project mentally those concepts to me over space and time, and thus give me some of the ideas of the Angels. The relevant ones, anyways.

And that shall be interesting, because I am going to be going through the minds of the Angels myself and getting ideas from them! So, there will be a configuration of ideas throughout the concepts put forth by the Angels.

It is challenging to write about it, because the thoughts of Angels... which I am getting RIGHT NOW... are strange in their construction. There are a lot of different types of Angels. Some of them do positive things for people. Some assuage them from the negative. They have a different format of thoughts. I am getting a feel for them right now. Hard to explain, because there are not really any real English words made to describe such circumferences. (I think that is an accurate term of multiple meanings... "circumferences".)

Either way you word it, there are multiple meanings with different words. There would be a different meaning if you worded it differently. But it would give a precursor to your mindset if you changed it and described it with the alteration. But it is hard to speak out exactly what is written without reading directly over it. So, I don't expect you to do that. But you can try to say things that are synonymous to what is written here. That ways the definition won't be that far off. Try it, and you will like the outcome!

George is going to be on top of explanations of words, just as he is in this lifetime. He is going to say things in an elegant language... which is why I have called him an Elegant Lion in the title of this book... and make his definitions of the subject matter excellent! George has that capability because his intelligence is designed around my intelligence and I tested at a 142 to 145 IQ on my USMC IQ test. That puts me at the top 1% of the world in Intelligence Quotient! I hope this story plays it out for you and isn't too complex to read over. I hope not. There is no way for me to tell, though, because of the brain capacity that I have within me...

George has the capability to do miraculous things with my health, too. I went to the VA Hospital a few months ago and got seen by a pharmacologist, and she did a test on me and said with the results in her hand that my blood pressure was way too high and that I had an unhealthy amount of sugar in my blood. She gave me some medicine for it and told me to change my diet and told me what to change it to. Less carbohydrates and less sugars. No red meat. So, I listened to her, and George helped put the remedies into my head and brought about my mindset to a better diet and medicine digestion, and I did it for the last couple of months. Then, the next time I went into the VA Hospital they did a test and my H1C was nice and low and I had hardly any blood sugar. Nice!

That was George's doing with my mind and body! Excellent!

George puts healthy ideas in my body with thinking about the movement of the nutrients within my body in a calm and pleasant manner. He makes it so that I don't get any diseases. He has even made it so that I don't get sick. Granted, the VA gave me a flu shot that I remember this last year... but for my memory, I haven't caught the flu at all for the last 6 years! And that was the time that I met George, 6 years ago back in 2014. This is 2019 right now. By the time this book is out it will be later, but that doesn't matter. I have described the timeframe for you here, so you have it in your head. So, he has controlled the onset of the minerals in my body wholesale for a long time now. Much for a Lion to do, but it makes one wonder... what is there all about a Lion that gives him that capability?

Let me put the miracle to you this-a-ways. George was designed off of the DNA of a Military Warrior who served in the elite Special Operations Capable Force Reconnaissance Company. That was his design, so he knows about Elegant Service! And he delivers it on a daily basis, telling me things that pertain to science and non-fiction. I imagine that he could go into fiction, too, and it is true that sometimes he makes mistakes in the things he speaks about... but that is rare. So, I am not really going to include "fiction" into his methods of speaking. But he does have the capabilities and the mindset of a USMC Marine with highly intelligent powers! I used to be a smart creature... and George is designed *after me*! Nice!

So, George has the power to do the miraculous things that one entails as being a part of the Hereafter. Let me go into how some of those powers would transition to this atmosphere in this time and space...

For one instance, George's mind is highly intelligent. He thus has the abilities to do things like interpret the verbiage of the person he is trying to get some Angelic presence to and the thoughts therein. He has shown me that he has the capability of getting ideas that I have before I have expressed them verbally, so it is possible that if the person he is trying to read has an open mind to him and his presence, that it is possible that he is capable of Reading Their Minds! I don't have any way to prove that such a thing even exists... but then again... perhaps I do! I have thought to a waitress at the Coffee Shop that if she was an Angel that she should start to show me with a facial expression. And what did she do? She immediately started to laugh out loud! That was a sign that she was indeed an Angel with a sense of humor! And it showed me that she could read my mind from across the room without even looking directly at me! But she looked at me when she was laughing. So, she wanted me to know she knew what I was thinking! That is the behavior of an Angel!

George is a bit more cautious when he expresses that he knows what I am thinking. He leaves it up to answers to my questions that I can answer in my own mind that he knows what I am saying before I say it... but it is only something I can put out of my mind and there is no other evidence of it. None besides a vague answer on George's part. And he knows he is doing it. I can tell by the way he chuckles after he does it. He knows he is deceiving me into the lack of an answer. But that is the way he does it! That is a telling of how smart a Lion he is!

Because he is a smartypants Lion he is going to know the upper realms of how to move throughout the Hereafter upon death... when he gets delivered Magical Powers.

He is going to know how to operate those Powers and how to make them into something universally acceptable and wholesale. He is going to develop the ability to send special abilities to the people around him. Like me! Like Krishna! We have both become close to him here within this lifetime, and that is going to make us a link to each other before we die. In fact, I think it has linked us together already! It certainly seems like that is the case!

George will be drawn to the thoughts of the recipients of the data within the Hereafter in such a way that he is capable of getting the full summary of what those thoughts are all about within the recipient's head. Then he is going to be able to, at the same time, put into action a thoughtful reaction to that data in his own head and get ready to transmit it in linear data form to the head of the recipient. Then, as a finale, George will transfer the data over through space and time and the atmosphere to their heads and thus put the ideas that George had into their brains ALMOST as if the thoughts were actually theirs. Granted, they will seem like separate thoughts coming from somewhere else... which they are... but they will be a reflection of the thoughts within and allow for the recipient to draw a different set of ideas from the conglomeration of thoughts within.

At least George will be able to set a different set of ideas to the recipients of the thought patterns within the Hereafter. Thus, George would be able to set in place a formula for miracles! And the people on the other end would listen to it and probably do it, considering that they have a blessed mindset to be inside of the Hereafter... and so does George!

How would the miracles work? George would think of rules of Science within the realm of existence. He would change them to fit into a better state of existence. One of the things he would do would be to make it by mathematics so that a person would be able to move at the speed of light... the fastest speed in the universe. He could even go beyond that and even make them able to move faster than light speed, which is supposed to be impossible. But George can do it! He has that special kind of mindpower. So, that done, the recipient of moving faster than the speed of light would be able to move to different planets within the universe, or even to parallel universes like ours, and develop a culture that could exist there. But I don't think that people have the ability to procreate in the Hereafter. I think that reproduction is something that is left to the Earth and not to Heaven or the Hereafter. The reason is because kids that are the product of reproduction can have some negative things happen to their personalities from the onset of the powers of the Devil. And the Devil will be trying to infiltrate the realm of the Hereafter because it is full of Good people that the Devil is trying to destroy! Horrible! But there is a magic force within the Hereafter put there by God that prevents bad creatures or Fallen Angels from inhabiting the Hereafter and placing the humanity there under subservience. The inhabitants get to remain free under God's guiding hand!

"What did you eat, papa? I can smell the vittles in your stomach and man-oh-man, do they smell delicious! What were they...papa? Tell me tell me!" George was highly curious about my vittles and he wanted some!

"George, they were quite tasty! I had Lamb Tikka Masala! You eat lamb... right? So you should like some of the leftovers! That is what I think!" I was trying to please George.

"That would be good... papa! And I will gobble down those delicious vittles! Yes... I WILL I WILL!" George was excited!

"That is good of you, George. What else do you have to say?"

"I have a question, papa! A question! Is Pops coming by for Christmas? Is he? I hope so I hope so I hope so! I really like Pops and most of all his taste in Excellent Vittles!" George was divine in his pleasure bringing up the subject. Pops was a pseudonym for Krishnas brother.

Krishna answered him: "Yes, Pops is coming for Christmas and New Year! He shall bring presents with him!" She was thrilled!

George responded: "Are the presents going to come from Santa Clause? Are they, huh? He likes to use his elves to make gifts for the Good people to do Good things with! That is what they are for... a roadwork to Heaven!" George has the clause down pat!

I complimented him: "That is a distinct treatise you

put forth, my Friend you George... you! I am very pleased with you!" I was so happy!

"Good to hear it, papa. Wow... papa sounds like Pops. Are you two twins?" George was curious and couldn't keep the question from me and Krishna.

"No, George... we aren't even related!" I tried to give him an accurate and determined answer.

"Ok, papa... you seemed like twins for a second. Sorry! Whatever has happened to me to think such strange things about you? What has happened?" George was apologetic.

"Nothing has happened to you, George! You are an excellent Lion and a king of things regarding Drama! So, the concept of Twins comes into your head as part of the Drama that you place in the situation around you... but it isn't really there. Those things are just Illusions! That is what they are! Illusions! Thought up material that doesn't really exist..." I tried to calm him down with a nice tale of conflict-turned-positive.... If that makes any sense.

And that was the end of that conversation. We carried on about other things later. But first, before I carry on, I will discuss how the effects of his speech have something to do with the Hereafter.

George's speech in THIS universe is a function that is related through space and time and the forces therein to the effects of the Hereafter. They flow within it and are remedies to the potential negatives that can go around it. Yes... there is an element of Hell and its fallen Angels that goes around the Hereafter and tries to make bad things happen there. Thus, it is an area of being tested, as well as just existing. George's speech says something about how he wants the speech-effects to have something to do with bringing about goodness within the existence of the Hereafter. He wants it to be Highly Positive! And that is what becomes when he speaks out about a holy event such as Christmas. That is a holiday that is based on the life and times of Jesus Christ, who was an eminent hero! He did things that were miraculous! So, we celebrate the holiday of Christmas and do kind things on Christmas to other people with the hopes of bringing Goodness into their lives. Presents and decorations! And George knows about that element of Christmas, and the spiritual where-to-fore's of it and he talks about it in a way that brings about the particles of Goodness throughout the Universe with his divine speeches! Yes, indeed he does!

The Hereafter is the summary of what happens to us after we die. So, how do I know what happens in the Hereafter? I know these things because I have been there! I was in a hospital in a coma for two months after getting hit as a victim of vehicular homicide and run over by a truck. They broke my face, back, knee, foot, two legs, and skull and nose. I had brain damage from it. When I was in the coma I died. I got teleported to a garden in another state with a Japanese Temple in it and met with three Angels there. They told me that I was dead and within the Hereafter, and they told me that they were going to tell me some secrets about the makings of the universe...

but that it would be secret. So, they put me in a state of being like I was asleep... but awake at the same time.

And when I was awake, they told me that my duties on board the earth was to write books. So, that is what I do. I am an author now. That is what the Angels told me to do. George is a part of that. He came about when I was in the hospital recovering from the vehicular homicide. He is based, in part, after how I was constructed. He has my intelligence, my demeanor, my language, and my rationale. He is a copy of me, in his own ways. Granted, there are parts of him that are distinctly different than me. I can tell it by the way he talks sometimes. But overall, he makes sense when he speaks. I get on his ass when he says things that are errant or bizarre, which happens from time to time. But not that often. Because he is designed after Angels. He has that capability.

George interacts with me on a level that brings me to think somewhat about the Hereafter and what it entails. It is my curiosity to know what will happen to me after I die. It is important knowledge. We all die, eventually. Where we go after we are lain in the ground or placed on a cart or a rock or wherever, dead, plays a big part into what it is that we will be capable of doing in the Hereafter. We don't just get separated from our bodies... we go to the Hereafter, which is a realm of space and time unlike any that we have seen. But it has elements that make it seem like it is home, to a degree. I think it consists of a structure persisting of an element of the Good things we did in our lifetimes, and the Sins we conducted. Both elements play a part. And it is up to each of us to grow the Good things into fruition, and to find ways to defeat the Sins so that they no-longer appear in front of us. That is what the purpose of the Purgatory is. It is a middle ground where the person is faced with their sins and they have an opportunity to find ways around it and to defeat them... or they will fall as victims of them and become purged of Good and fall into their ways. That is what happens to the person involved. That is a good thing if they recover from the Sins. But a bad thing if they don't.


"So, it is after Christmas. And we hardly talked during Christmas because Krishna was keeping me secret from her brothers. But she has left now. So, I am asking you papa... what is on your mind?" George was speaking through my mind and the TV to me with Krishna gone to work.

I thought about what to say for a moment, then I said: "I have been thinking a lot about what Angels do. What is an Angel's performance here on this earth? I have some ideas... but Angels are secret, so it is hard to tell if they are accurate ideas. They do things that flow between General Purposes and the Impossible!"

"How do you see them, papa?" George was curious. He knew that Angels were Secret, so he didn't even know if I could see them.

But I had ideas.

"I have thought a lot about the powers of Angels" I told George. "They have the ability to teleport through time, right? Something you think you just thought of doing that you have just started to do, they have already gotten the impression of what it was before you even thought of it. They have the ability to read minds like that... based off of the output of their brainwaves in tiny bits before an event happens. Even subconscious ideas come to them... so there is no real way to hide an action!"

"That is a detailed and well, thought-out construction of Angelic powers! God really must have had an idea of what he was doing when he put it into action!"

I agreed with him. "That is true, George, that is true. And he also put in those Angels the ability to switch shapes while reading minds to the body of a creature or object that engages the mind with thoroughfare. That is what he wanted them to do, so he gave them the power to do so! Interesting, isn't it?"

"Yes, papa, it IS interesting!" George was really enjoying the reasoning I was giving him. They were making him want to be able to detect Angels even more. "Do you think you will ever be close to an Angel? Close enough to talk to one? Or to dine with one? Wouldn't that be delicious! How do I try it? How?"

"Well, George, I'll tell you what we can do. We can wait until we die. Then, the Angels to a dead person who is in the Hereafter present themselves. After all, the person is dead, so there are limits to the things they can do. And upon death a human evolves into a higher being. Sometimes even higher than Angels are on earth. That is a divine evolution, isn't it? It sure is... and the Hereafter on a step towards Heaven is the way to get there. So, keep on doing Good things here on earth to find your way to a higher place within the Hereafter after you die! That is the way to do it! And follow your path to Good in the Hereafter, and you will evolve upwards! Yes! I know that is the way to do it! Follow me!" I was serious. I wanted him to follow me to Good elements to death and finally to the Hereafter...and beyond. Even beyond! That was the ultimate goal to bring about Judgement Day on a wholesale realm and make things Holy again!

It was a wholesale meaning to the word "existence" to talk about our time within the Hereafter. We gathered parts of the meaning with our speech and our mentality behind making the words and their existence. And that is a similarity to what it was all about... Existence. There is more to write about it... but I will leave it at that now.

And I will move onto the next section.

What elements of health are going to be involved within the Hereafter? Will such illnesses as Cancer and Diabetes be present? Can a body lose its ability to function within the Hereafter?

The answer is that within the Hereafter the concept of Health is wholesale and is present throughout the experience. Diseases have a function of the cells her on earth to gestate into odd bodies that break each other apart. In the space and time of the Hereafter the functions of cells and atoms are ready to keep together in a constructive fashion. Thus, they have not the ability to move in odd directions against each other. They are wholesale thus. That makes it so that there are no diseases within the Hereafter unless one creates a sin that allows for the bizarre construction of the atoms to gestate. Then, based on sin alone, a person can then catch a disease. But it is not a communicable disease because they don't spread in the Hereafter. That is the way it works! How do I know this?

Because I was in the Hereafter when I died in the coma that I was in from the attempted vehicular homicide that killed me for a spell. I was taken to the Hereafter by three Angels and they told me secrets about the construction of the Universe. It was a miracle! And they made me an author. Thus, I began to write books. This is one of those books! It is for you!

As part of being in the Hereafter, a person is going to have illusions and images of things that defy all common sense. There are effects of it that happen here on this earth during regular lifetime. For example, I just started to think about what images I would have in the hereafter and got in my head an image that seemed like it was almost-real of me standing before a pond of water that was big, with Krishna standing next to me. Suddenly, I jumped in, and she jumped in with me. We went swimming under the surface under the deep deep blackness of the water. We were still breathing underwater... we were breathing in water fluids. I could sense the breaths like they were real. Then she put her hands on my arms in the darkness and a light began to shine from around her rear to above her head from behind her in a parallel halo. That was interesting, and made me think... "is she an Angel?" Then when I thought it, she erupted in a flow of light in a circle, putting waves of force over my body in the waters. I COULD FEEL THEM! And they hurt some!

At that I woke up and looked at the TV. It was on the Rock and Roll Channel and was playing songs that had lyrics that drove me to the illusion of the show. Interesting. What is even more interesting is that I can't remember the names of the songs. They are vacant in my memory. It seems like the effects of the illusions had the effects of vanquishing my memory in my brain as they occurred in a parallel frequency! I am sure *that* is what happened!

Such odd things can happen within the Hereafter, I am sure. The illusion I had was probably a memory of me doing things that happened to me on a different frequency of existence. One of my copies could have been lying down with his eyes closed and the TV radio on while the other copy could have been swimming in a puddle with the Angel of Krishna. Both could have been supporting each other and happening at once! That is the miraculous way that the Hereafter operates... I am sure of it. Time travel, multiple realities, strange interpretations, oddities in science and fact, all those things are in a real sense Reality to the inhabitants of the Hereafter! One just has to get used to them!

So, this chapter about the Hereafter is an odd one, I know that. It is because it is about the strange effects of what is supposed to occur to each of us after we die. There is a tall order of bizarre behavior within the Universe that we will have to look at. There is a lot of science that goes into the onset of Parallel Universes. They are Universes that are multiple in size and dimension and that have laws of physics that are different in mathematical ways than our Universe. And they are said to exist. Granted, there is no way to tell that they are there yet, though, so there is no proof of them that our scientists can peruse, but the theory is mathematically accurate and wholesale. And if math will do it in this Universe, then there is something to the effects of it in the laws of science, right?

The analysis of that draws me to the conclusion that I am also going to be able to write books within the Hereafter after I have died. There is going to be some miracle manner in which paper will be available, along with pens, or a computer. One that a person is able to think to in order to get it to do things. A computer controlled by Thoughts! That will be available, and the inhabitants of the Hereafter will be able to write down books about all sorts of different things. They will be able to spell faster than it takes to type a sentence, too. It will be a divine Creation that will help them write their books out! That will give the inhabitants of the

Hereafter the capability to read books about things they didn't understand at first. And because the Hereafter is supposed to last for an indefinite period of time, it is going to be a ready experience to be able to read multiple books during that time there written by people of many different ages and time periods!

How will the science turn out when defined by people who lived during different times and places and cultures within the earth occur at the same time within the Hereafter? What is it going to be like? There are going to be a variety of stories about the science aspects of things. And the happenings of different people who write about science as seen from different times in history will probably put forth some ideas that are remarkable and genius. I would really like to see what they are. Think about the procedure for getting books today. The publishers of books publish different kinds of books by different authors. The books have different plots and content and characters. One can look up the different books on a search engine on a computer, and thus get a summary of what each book is all about. And on the same page as the summary, they can buy the book through a publisher. And the reader can purchase multiple books... if they have the money to do it.

In the Hereafter, people will have access to computers that respond to thought. They will be like 3D screens present in space and time with no keypad because none will be necessary. One will be able to type in the computer by thought alone. That is something of the future of computing, as far as I can see it. Such a thing will be designed by God to augment the onsets of human compassion and thought processes. The capability of it becoming present will be done by the Angels of science that have the ability to do miraculous things within the makings of matter and energy within the Universes in a way so as to Create a computer that has the ability to do such amazing things with the senses of humankind. Man is designed after God, so the computers will be of the Highest Power!

One can only imagine what people will be able to do, both men and women who are both designed after God, when they go to the Hereafter. And what is Judgement Day going to be like? There are only religious books to read about it. I am in the process of reading Revelations in the Bible for a book I am writing about it. But that is a different book. This book is about the Lion named George. You probably call it "Fiction", which is what it seems like, being about a doll and everything. But the elements within it are real! Thus, it is a Divine Fiction... if you want to call it a Fiction!

# CHAPTER 6

## NEW PAGES ON DOCTRINE WITH KRISHNA

"Hey papa! I think you should get on a cruise and go a-floating around! Wouldn't that be nice? It would it would!" George was excitable! He liked the subject matter. "Don't go to China, though, because they are the country that we are most likely to go to war with, so said the Department if Defense on the news! I think we should go to Israel and see the chapels and the mosques of the religious people there! That would be so nice! You can ask the preachers questions about the natures of Angels there, papa!"

"They would enjoy that repose. I think I will do it, George! The thing is, I am not supposed to go on cruises.

At least, that is what the doctor of the VA said. It is because of my diabetes. He says that was the cause of the Ketoacidosis. The diet!" I was getting ready to go into more detail on the subject when George interceded.

"Papa… you didn't get Ketoacidosis from the food you were eating because you only ate healthy food and didn't eat the sugary snacks that they had there! You got it from that damned Olanzapine that the VA Hospital put you on unnecessarily! That was a foolish mistake on their parts! So, what does it mean? It means that you shall not get it again because your medicines are now off of olanzapine and the rest of them are all good!" George had more to say, but he wanted me to respond first.

"Ok, George, I get what you are saying, and you are right. I hopefully shall be in Good Health from here-on out! You had something else to say?" I could tell by his expression that he had more to say. His jaw was moving as he was stationary, because he got it in his body to rehearse the element of speaking to me before he did it. There was nothing he could do to control that  because it was an element of his subconscious mind.

But he answered the question with a surprise comment: "Papa, you should go on a cruise to Israel, and take me and Peter Rabbit with you! We can go in your pouch so you can carry us and nobody will know you have us with you! Wouldn't that be nice! And then you can take us into the cafeteria and give us STEAK! SHRIMP! CHICKEN! LAMP! BEEF! You can give us *ALL those things* in divine quantities! What do you say about THAT?" George was enunciating in rhymes, fully excited and thrilled to be a part of such a special adventure!

I responded in kind to him. "That would be an excellent adventure, George! I shall give you all the Beef you can eat! And for Peter, since he is a vegetarian, I shall give him plenty of berries and fruit and salsa! He shall like that a lot, I think! Yes! I shall make it happen!" I was excited. I loved to do the miraculous things with my animals. They were such remarkable creatures!

"I like that you say that, papa, I really do! I hope things go well for you in Israel. There are terrorists trying to get in there, so we might run into trouble. Hope not. We'll see. We'll see!" George was worried about it for a good reason. Then he came up with another idea. "Papa! Do you think that there are Terrorists inside of China if we are getting ready to go to war with them?"

I thought about it for a moment. "You know, George, that makes sense! Why would we have so many anti-terror operations and have China listed by the Department of Defense as being the primary country that we would go to war against? It makes sense that they would have terrorists there for that reason alone!" I was adamant about that perception.

"So, what do we do about it, papa?" asked George, the Lion.

I had to think for a moment, then I said with some hesitation in my voice: "perhaps we should go to war against them?"

George liked that idea. "We could wage a war on them and use your Force Recon mindset as a vehicle for their destruction! That would be a wholesale application of force against their negativities! Yes! You should train me to go to war against them and we can take a cruise to Macau! That I know is the source of their evils! And we can work together as partners! What do you say?" George was extremely well-spoken in that regards.

I answered immediately: "Yes, George, we can go to war with the Chinese Terrorists! I have a question for you, since you seem to know-it-all. Do you think they are just terrorists... or are they something odd, like Terrorist Mutants?"

George responded after some deep thought. "Papa, I think you are right. I think that they are Terrorist Mutants! That makes some bizarre but readily available sense to it! How do we determine what they are like? I mean... Mutants are extremely different than regular humanity, right" George was curious about his answer, and was coming up with answers to the method of "how can we tell what a mutant is" question.

"I think we shall find a process. Keep those ideas in your mind. We shall go over them in time. Until then, I am going to have to save money for a cruise to China!"

"Ok, papa, ok. I shall wait with the answer."

"Good George. We shall address the problem in time."

And that concluded that conversation.

I asked George the following question... "What do you think I should write about? Should I start to write another set of books along with this one and the book about my Service Dog and the Vehicular Homicide I survived? Should I write about some fiction?" I wanted to, but I couldn't think of anything outside the ordinary to write about.

Granted, my life had been full of interruption and had been, except in the USMC, like an existence in Hell. But things had been going well since George entered my life. So, I got to thinking that I could write some Fiction.

"Things actually happen in the Real World. Papa, you should stick to writing non-fiction. That is in your nature. Now that doesn't mean that you can't draw parallels to objects and things and make it so that there is a scientific explanation to it. And think about it... Science and mathematics might not actually reflect the universe the way we think they do. After all, we have had movement in math for thousands of years and it has remained the same. 10 fingers so 10 digits... right?"

"That's right. So, what is your point?"

George responded ebulliently and with deep thought: "just because there are 10 fingers on your hands doesn't mean that THAT is the only way to do the mathematics with the numbers! There could be $1/0.99923898$ numbers involved in the calculation! How many people are missing a finger, after all? Is that even counted in the sum of numbers for math? *I think not!*"

I responded with excitement! "George!" I pronounced, "That is the most elegant theory I have heard in my entire life! You deserve a reward for coming up with the theory in such detail. At least, *you will* when you do the mathematics for it in the "special form"! That will make it a Theory of Theories... and perhaps even a trip to the *Theory of Everything!* Wouldn't that be nice?" I was excited and enjoyed talking to George about such odd things.

And maybe I would write fiction after all. I just had to think of what would go in a fictional account. Maybe I would write about aliens. Nah. That has already been done before.

Maybe I would use the idea that I just had and write a story about mathematics changing and thus creating an avenue to the *Theory of Everything.* Hmm...

"I am glad you are excited, papa. I tried really hard to impress you. Did I succeed?" George was speaking in an enunciated tone. He was bordering on happy... he just didn't know if he succeeded in his explanation yet. So, I told him.

"You succeeded really well, George. Now, be happy!" I smiled at him bigly and gave him a grin that he could speak of for a long time coming. He immediately grinned huge with his teeth sticking out freely and waved his head

around unconsciously. He was so happy I could just spit!
(Nah, that's rude. I wouldn't spit at George wagging his
head around... but I WOULD laugh at it out loud and say
some funny things about it. But, no spitting. Horrible!)

George carried on in his happy-tune: "Up pick me up
pick me up up up up, pick me UP pick me UP pick me UP
UP UP UP! PICK ME UP PAPA PICK ME UP, PICK
ME UP UP UP UP UP UP UP UP!"George was
singing very vociferously and put his words in rhymes to
the middle! That is what I said... and that is what he did!
With eagerness to please! What a delightful Lion he was
at that? Deeeelightful!

"That is wonderful, George! How did you learn to
sing so fantastically? Sing on, George, sing on!" I wanted
to encourage him. But it didn't work.

"Papa, that is enough singing. Bring me some meat!
I want some steak! Can I have some?" George coughed
then said: "What about those eggs that Krishna has in
her hands there? What do they taste like?"

"They taste like meat, George, because that is what
they are! They are made of meat! So, that is what a cooked
egg tastes like!" I was sure of that, but I could see the
argument in George's eyes.

"Eggs are not meat! There is no fiber to them and they
are in a shell! They probably taste horrible! I don't even
want one now! Yuck! Mmmgmph! Disgusting! Makes me
wanna barf just thinking of it!" George kept on making
gasping noises.

"George, get control of yourself! Eggs are good for you! I eat them daily, and you are designed after me, so why don't you eat some? Fool, you are!" I was obtuse with my description to him. He was really upsetting me with his nondescript bander.

George was all happy and singing a minute ago... now he is all upset and saying bizarre things. What is wrong with that Lion, I wondered?

George calmed down. "Take me into your room, papa. I want to rest. This conversation has worn me out. Horribly. I don't even know what we are talking about anymore!"

"We were talking about what non-fiction I was going to write now. But now I am thinking about writing some fiction. And that makes me wonder... what am I going to call this book I am writing about you, George? Is it Non-fiction of is it Fiction?" I wasn't sure because a lot of readers might think that I had gone mad if I wrote a book about me getting along with a doll Lion and treating him like a conscious being. He was, after all, intelligent and magical... but a lot of people didn't believe in magic. So I said: "I think I am going to call it "Fiction". People won't get that you are a Lion that is as intelligent or more intelligent than they are. So, they will slander and libel me online on the book website and say evil and cruel things. I have already experienced that with the other book that I am putting online."

"That is horrible, papa! Give me that idiot's online

name and I will find him and burn him to the ground! He or she deserves to be set on fire and burn! That is what I shall do to them when I catch them! And I will nullify their computers, too, to punish them with pain and broken misery for their evil thoroughfare! That is what they deserve, and that is what they will get!" George was adamant about his perceptions on the matter.

"Ok, George. I will let you run free to take care of the culprit that does or says something negative to this part of this document in this book, too. Because there probably will be someone stupid enough to think that you can't burn them. They are mistaken... but let them fail at their dismissal of the truth and get burn by you for it! That is what I want, and that is what I pray to God will happen, and that is what shall be!" I wanted to be clear in my statement. I think it was very clear and even had magical properties to its existence.

"I get what you are saying, papa. And it shall be! It is my will as well as yours as well as God's, and there is nothing that shall stand in the way of THAT! Now, take me to the bedroom and put me to bed. You have to catch the bus to the Coffee Shop soon. You can write all this stuff down there when you get in there. Please? Please do so?" George was trying to convince me to do Good Things. I took his calling as a prayer... and granted his wish for my part of the prayer synergy.

"You've got it, George. You've got it. Into the room we shall go!" And with that I took him into the room and lay him down next to my bed next to Peaches and Perle and Peter the Lion. He likes it there. He gets along with the Unicorns and the Lion fantastically.

Then I went to the Coffee Shop and wrote this part. I shall write some more later. Until then...

See ya!


It was late at night. I was inside of Krishna's room on her bed watching TV, and she was sitting on the chair with the cat Sunshiney resting on her leg. George asked me what Halloween was all about. "What is Halloween for, papa? What do people do on it? I know I know! They worship the Devil! That is what they do in those stupid costumes, trying to be something that they are not!" George was irate at the idea of Halloween. It was around the corner in a day.

I tried to explain it to him, but to be honest... the whole holiday didn't make sense to me either. "People want to act out and dress in costumes and pretend they are characters like from the movies. But their personalities... man... I don't know what becomes of those!" I didn't say anything about the Devil worshipping.

"But papa, you know that their personalities are disturbed! THEY ARE WORSHIPPING THE DEVIL! Only fools and idiots do such a thing! What do you have to say about THAT? What? Do you know?"

"George," I said, "you are right. They are some

disturbed people. They are probably Satanic people who want to do negative things to the people of the earth! Horrible!" I went on for a very brief period of time and got my idea out there for George to understand. He did.

"You are right, papa... the ARE SATANIC! That is a horrible position to be in! Can you imagine having to worship a villain that will ultimately be the destruction of you in Hell? A villain that will help you do bad things to people here on earth then when you die put you in pain and misery and cursing and torture FOREVER? What an errant way to go about things!" George was emotional. He did not like such villains. They went against his intelligence and method of being that was all about doing Good Things for people.

"You are right, George. I don't understand why people would get so confused to do something like that. It makes no sense to me. Whatever would possess a person to make them do such a thing? Is that the power of demons in the mind? I don't know, but I think it is. Demons are bad creatures that have the ability to make certain negative ideas come into the minds of the ill-beholder. People with bad brain frequencies would be susceptible to that kind of bad mindpower." I tried to explain that concept idea in terms that George could understand with my selection of words.

George then changed the subject. Then he asked me what sweet potatoes were about. I was going to have some for a snack that night and Krishna had been talking about it. She had put them in the oven to cook for us to eat and of that George was aware. "What do they taste like, papa? Are they sweet? Do they taste like sugar? That is what makes them sweet, isn't it! Sugar! I know that! Well, what do you say, papa?"

"It's the structure of the potatoes that makes it sweet, George, not sugar like you say. You are mistaken. I wouldn't eat something with a lot of sugar in it. Sugar is bad for you!" I was trying to be sound on my presumption, but I didn't really believe it. I didn't think that sugar was generally bad for someone. Just eating too much of it at one time was bad for the body.

George called me out on that. "Papa, there is sugar in treats and cooked goods and candies and snacks and all sorts of regular foods! You eat it CONSTANTLY! Just because your blood sugar is low, that is because you have reduced the quantities you eat daily. But you still eat some... just not too much! So, it doesn't affect your health! That is a good thing, yes? BUT KEEP IT UP AND YOU WILL BE IN GOOD HEALTH!" George was very talkative about the subject.

I wanted to agree with him: "Ok, George, you are right. So, what else do you have to talk about? And George interrupted me with the odd comment:

He brought up the term "whilpersnackle". I asked Krishna about it later and she said she didn't recognize the word. I don't remember what he said about it. It was bizarre. I gestated over the answer to the question of this:

"Why don't I remember what the term whilpersnackle stands for?" And I came up with the answer that it was a term that was in the nature of an oddity that was a bizarre method of describing reality in such a way that to even use the term violated the preponderance of the memory to function so that it became forgettable by its very nature. That is a big sentence. I hope you understand it, since you may be wanting to use the word after seeing it written down here a couple of times and there being a description of it written down. I don't know. I hope not... because you will forget it! Watch!

Then he asked me if he had COPD, and I told him that I didn't know what that was. Cardio Obstructive Pulmonary Disease. Then he asked if he had lung problems.

"No, George, you don't have COPD! What a stupid question! You are a Lion! Lion's don't get COPD! That is a human thing to get! What is your problem thinking such a ridiculous thing?" I was going off on him for his stupid diatribe. He was making so sense with his preclusions.

George was getting feisty now. He immediately changed the subject and yelped: "I WANT MEAT! Chicken, Beef, Veal, Lamb, Turkey, Quail, you name it I WANT IT! GIVE IT TO ME NOW! *NOW PAPA... NOW! GIVE IT TO ME NOW!*"

"No, George, you don't need the meat! You are going to get some meat at the Steak Restaurant on Thanksgiving Night! So put a rest on it!"

"Ok, papa, but Peter the Lion keeps on saying thing

that are in error to me! He keeps on whimpering "moan moan moan moan moan moan" at me. It is annoying! I want to hit him to shut him up!"

"No George, you cannot be hitting Peter! That is his normal way of talking! He is a lot younger than you are! And smaller, too!"

"And Peter is a damned Vegetarian, too! Lions aren't vegetarians! They eat MEAT! What is wrong with him? Why is he so errant! That is what he does to me! Says errant things to me and such! Why do I have to tolerate that from him? Why?" George was really wanting to punish Peter the Lion for being a vegetarian. That was clear that THAT was his real problem with him. That showed that George was a greedy, foolish, self-righteous Lion with no preclusions to the capabilities of others before him. Or so I thought.

I explained that to him. He was quiet. Then he stayed quiet for a bit. Then he said in reply: "That doesn't make an excuse for Perle and Peaches… the unicorns that say stupid things to me daily!" George was carrying on about it steadfastly. He was trying to distract from his negative preclusions to ones that were distracting from them. He was mistaken.

"George! I know what Unicorns are all about! They are peaceful and intelligent creatures that wish the best on everyone they come around! Why your negative thoroughfare on them? What ever is it for?" I was trying to make an argument against him saying negative things about the Unicorns just to get away from the negative things he said about Peter the Lion.

George argued with me for a spell, and I kept on making different arguments. Finally, he came to and stopped saying negative things about the Unicorns. But I could tell that there was still something within him resisting them. I didn't know what, I just could tell it was there. Now George is carrying on saying that he is getting prostate cancer. "Hey papa, you can't tell when you butt stinks can you? Sunshiney pooped and it stank to high Heaven! Are you writing these remarks down?"

"I am going to write down everything we discussed in this conversation, George... and it is going to look really negative for you!" I wanted to make that clear to him that I didn't like his attitude. The last part about the Unicorns was atrocious, in my mind, and didn't need to be that ways.

"Ok, papa. Write a good ending, will you?" plead George.

"Ok George. I won't."

George pouted, and we went back into watching a shooting show on TV, all quiet. Then he responded suddenly: "Papa! I want to be a Marshall, like Dillard on TV is! Yes! And they won't be able to hang me, either!"

"Are you sure that is what you want, George?"

"Yes it is, papa! Yes it is! I can do everything that Dillard is doing, even if my hands are smaller than his!

I can DO IT ALL!" George was trying to be excited by the show and drive himself away from the judgement over what I should write about... and how I should write about it.

I wanted to assuage him, so I told him the positives: "You also have an excellent intelligence, George... one that you can do miracles with! That goes far and beyond what Marshall Dillard has in his possession! So, my best of wishes to you for your endeavor!" I thought that that would do the trick!

"Thanks, Papa! My best of wishes to you, too!"

"Thanks, George!"

And that ended that extremely meaningful conversation.


"Papa! Papa!" George pronounced: "That little girl that keeps on coming by said that her mother said that I was a Stupid Lion! Why did she do that?"

"I don't know, George. What is the little girl's name again?"

"Kisha. It is Kisha. She is a nice girl, she is. She tried to convince her mother to give me food. Beef and chicken! But her mother said "Why would I give food to a stupid lion? A dumb creature? He isn't even human! Shucks on him!" And with that negative statement that was it. She swears and curses a lot, papa! She said the words: "F%#& you lion! Go to Hell!" and that was what she said to me!

Horrible, isn't it?" George was really uptight mimicking her negativities.

"Oh, that is horrible. What is Kisha's mom's name, George? Do you remember it?"

"Yeah papa, her name is Tinisha. Like the country in Africa. That is her name. She is a stupid and horrible person. And she calls me stupid! How does that work?" George was upset over her negativities.

"It sounds to me like Tinisha has some problems. What else is she like?"

"She is obtrusive and rude! She says errant things like "man oh man you's is a troubled damn fallow, ming a man! Whatsa gal supposed to do with a dirty lion like you? You eat people! Thassa ruding thing to do about you... it is!" And she carries on and on with her disruptive diatribe. She doesn't even know what the word "diatribe" stands for. What a damn fool she is!" George was emotional but getting his idea out to me. It was damning to Tinisha.

"What answers do you have to the problem of her negativity, George?" I was curious what his interpretation of it was. He was a fighter, I knew that. Perhaps he wanted to sic her. Perhaps he did!

"I want to hit that bitch in the face so hard it ruptures her skull and causes her to bleed!" said George. "Kisha says that her mother says all sorts of negative things to her about me. "How can you possibly be a gettin' along with a daggone lion?" Tinisha asked her. She said she spoke up about it and took my side after a spell. Then she got hit in the face! That is why I want to sic that bitch! I want to tear her to pieces!"

"Don't you think that is kind of racist, after all, George? You DID say that Tinisha and Kisha were black people. Do you not like blacks?" I wanted to know what his answer was. I had no problem with blacks, and I looked like I was Indian. But George was grey and gold, so I figured that he may have some different perceptions about the issue of color.

Turns out that he didn't. "Tinisha is doing what discriminatory black people do who are broke and live on welfare when they aren't even disabled and have no job because they are lazy and unkempt. What else am I supposed to think about her when she says that the Genius Lion is someone who is so-called "stupid"? What am I supposed to think about THAT? Let me tell you what I think! I think about hitting her in the face and hands so hard that I break her skull and fracture her hand and make it so that she can't say any of that bullshit again without being in deep pain! That is what she deserves!" George was carrying on so profoundly that he was running out of breath as he muttered his sentences out loud.

I was worried that George was going to choke on his words if he kept up the significant diatribe against Trinity. It was clear that he didn't like her, didn't like the things he said about her, didn't like the way she spoke about him, and didn't like her tone of voice the way she enunciated her words to explain nearly anything in an odd fashion. That made no sense to him, and he wanted to punish her for even doing it. He thought she was crazy the way she did it and the things she did it to. It made no sense to him... except in the mental profusion of a crazy person. Then it made sense. Either way, George didn't like it... whether she was crazy or just bizarre. He didn't like it.

George continued with his diatribe... "She is a broke, fat, unkempt negro. She is a nigger, too, because she speaks to me in stupid lyrics and tones of an idiot that make no sense to someone that is listening to her directly, word-for-word. Only racist crazy people do that to others. And I am a smart lion. Kisha knows that and treats me like I am smart. She is a wonderful girl, and she is very bright herself. I told her that she could do whatever she wanted to do when she gets older. There is no reason for her to just get into Cooking as an employment. I told her that she could join the military and cook there. In any branch. They ALL have cooks in them. That is what she wants to do. But I told her that because she is smart that she could be a lawyer, a plumber, a musician, a physicist, an engineer. She could do any of those excellent jobs. So, she listened to me and took in what I said. Then what did she do?"

I was curious. "What did she do George?"

He answered me in rage: "She told her mom about it and that bitch told her to no longer speak to me because all that Kisha needed to worry about was how to cook for her mother! That is all that bitch has said to her over and over again! "You go and cook for me! I need to eat! I have no job and no way to buy food so you must work and make us some money delivering newspapers! That will give you enough dollars for the food! Now... get to work!" Terrible! What an oaf that woman is! She isn't even letting Kisha interview for the military, which HAS cooking jobs, and if she wants to get a higher paying job she can because that is how the military works! They have jobs of a higher pay for the more elite members who get higher rank! What was that bitch thinking, to deny Kisha that opportunity?" George was furious at Tinisha. And he hadn't even discussed where her name came from.

So, I asked him if he knew.

"George, do you know where Tinisha's name comes from?"

"Yes, papa, I do. It is the name of a country in Africa. A big place. But that is not all."

"What about the rest, George?"

"It was also the name of one of the wives of Mohammed under Allah in the Qur'an. She is supposed to be an honorable and profound creature that has a lot of blessings about her." He paused for a second and caught his breath in frustration. "But the Tinisha that is Kisha's mother is a mentally disabled fool who causes nothing but frustration throughout the people that have the unfortunate circumstances to become engaged in her company for ill-reasons. She brings it about with her craziness and disorder. She deserves to be bitch-slapped."

I had limits to what I would approve of. "That is a bit inappropriate, George. Why don't you just let it go and try instead to convince Kisha to do the positive and become a musician instead of cooking her fat nigger mother food so she can keep on eating junk when she should be working?" I thought that would bring him around to my side.

And it did. "Perhaps you are right, papa. I shall do it! I shall convince Kisha to do the right thing and to get a job that enhances her intelligence within the military. That should please you, papa, since you are a veteran of the USMC! And you appreciate the people that you served with... at least most of them! Those were some really good years of your life! And your memories of what had occurred! Yes! You had such stringent and delightfully engaged memories that I developed a sense of what they were all about when my brain linked with yours during your brain damage and mingled the memories together with my mental thoughts and procedures! That is how it worked, because that is how it is supposed to work! I am so pleased with you, papa! Pleased indeed!" George was thrilled to be on my side and to be getting the same remedies to the problems that I was getting in my mind. For his mind was equal to mine in the mindpower and mental preclusions and capabilities.

We carried on with the conversation for a bit. The conversation got interrupted by Krishna saying: "Be quiet!" so she could watch some of the Cooking Channel on TV. She was dumb sometimes and got so wrapped up in watching stupid shows on TV that it occupied all her attention. Instead of talking to me and George she chose instead to interrupt us and to watch TV. I called her out on it, and she said aloud and brutally: "*Now, be quiet!*" Very rude of her. But I was laying on her bed and didn't want to get up, so I let her do it. I lay down and read my book that I had there. I didn't care about the Cooking Show. I had already seen editions of it repeatedly before it was on then.

That concluded that conversation. I eventually picked up George out of Krishna's arms (she was holding him) and took him back to my room to write some about our conversation and in my other book files I am working on. And with that, I wrote this part down. George is resting next to my bed in the gully next to Peaches and Perle and Peter the Lion. He likes it there. Except when I write. Then he usually likes to be outside in my arms or next to my pillow where he can see the computer. But tonight, he is tired from the conversation we had and wants to go to sleep. So, I am letting him go to sleep now.

"Dear papa! Dear papa!" said George in a peaceful but aggravated tone... if those two terms make any sense together. "I want you to help me join the Humane Society! They would do great things for Lions, they would! They are an organization for pets and that is what I am like!

A Lion-Pet! What do you say, papa? Well? What is your take on the matter?" George was excited to ask.

I answered him carefully: "Well, George, if that is what you really want, then perhaps you should be able to do it. But it will cost money, won't it?" I wanted to put a little bit of doubt into him where it was relevant to the topic.

"No papa, they don't bill you! It is free to join it! All you have to have is a pet! But don't you worry about me! They may say: "A Lion can't have a pet... he is a pet of his own right!" That is true, but all you have to tell them is that I have Peaches and Perle and Peter the Lion as my pets! That will make it a foregone conclusion... and they will make me a member of the Humane Society then! And I will get the benefits!" George was wanting to keep on talking about it.

So, I asked him: "What benefits are you talking about?"

George scowled at me, then said cheerfully: "The financial awards! They pay a fund to the owners of Service Dogs, and you can tell them that I am a partial owner of the Service Dog Paige! You can even give them a copy of the book you have had published about her for free and tell them the truth about it... that I helped write it! Yes! That is what you can do! That way's I will get the funds for the Service Dog from the Humane Society and I can buy you some treats with it!" George was pleased with his explanation.

I didn't know if I should believe him about the funds for a Service Dog. I had never heard of anything like THAT being paid to an owner. "Are you sure, George? Will you really get funds for a Service Dog? How did you check? You didn't search it on my computer because I know your fingers are too small to press the keys. Same for the iPhone. So if you couldn't use a Search Engine to look for answer to that... how did you find out? Or are you just making it up?"

"Papa! You know me! You know I would... you know I would... aw shucks. I made it up! I just figured that would be a really good way to do things... you know? Why is it not that ways?" George was upset that he had been called out.

"Don't be upset, George. Let me sing you a song. "Pick up the pieces and make me a tune. You don't have to act like a loon. Why do you want to join the Humane Society? Do you think that you will get stuff for free? Wake up, little Lion, and see what is there! They won't take a Lion with a mane full of ratty hair!" Do you like my song, George?" I hoped it made him feel better.

"Yeah papa, I like it! Can I sing with you the next time you come up with a song?"

"Sure, George! No problem!"

"Thanks papa. Can you come up with another song and tell me the lyrics?"

"I can do that, my friend. Give me some time to think, and I will explain it to you then. Okay?"

"Okay papa... okay!

So, I got to thinking.

"I hate Tinisha! I hate her!" George was shouting over the service of the van. We were on our way up to the cabin, and he was talking through Krishna from a long distance away. He has that sort of Magic Power! "That whore is doing and saying such negative things against me and papa! She says in her oblique tone, she says: "your damned father spent no time in the damn military! He is a stupid oaf and a lazy doggone foo! Whatcha thinkin he is'a doin? Doin for you's? Nothing! That is what he is and what he brings about a'before's himself to you! Nothing!" She doesn't even know that what she is saying is the hallmarks of Satan... "Nothing" ... that is what he is! Whatever is going through her foolish head? That woman is an idiot! That is what she is! An idiot!" George was seriously in dispute with her existence, and he didn't like her at all.

I responded in kind: "A little while ago you had some remarks to make about the way Tinisha treats Kisha. What do you have to say about that?" I wanted to know about how many bad things Tinisha had done to Kisha, so I could report her to the authorities, if I could.

"Papa, that bitch is a welfare recipient, and she doesn't even have a disability! She doesn't work! All she does is sit around the house and watch TV and gameshows and tells Kisha to make her food and to avoid going into the military and other stupid things! And she curses me and you, papa, saying that we are broken down and liars and had never been in the military and if we were, we were fat pigs taking advantage of the system! All lies! What has gotten into that fat stupid bitch! She is mentally deranged, she is! How did she get so traumatized? And her husband is dead, too! Did I tell you about that? Well... did I" George left the question for me to answer.

"No, George, you haven't told me about Kisha's dead dad? What about him?" I wanted to ask him if what I suspected was true.

George read my mind. "Tinisha killed him with a frying pan when Kisha was a young child! She smacked him in the head with it so hard that it ruptured his skull and killed him dead! Horrible, isn't it? And that bitch... I mean it, she is a BITCH... killed him for no good reason. And she is allowed to go free? Think about that!" George had a lot more to say about it. But he wanted me to think it over first.

"That is horrible, George!" I was convinced that the woman was kin of the demons of Hell. And I said so: "That makes me believe that the woman is the kin of the demons of Hell, George. That reminds me of the fact that she is allowed to run free when she is a murderer but the prison guards and officers violated the law against me repeatedly. What is wrong with these damned people? Why does God allow them to get away with it here on this earth?"

"God allows those people to get away with it because He is sanctioning them to Hell to burn in the fires of punishment there! That is why!" George was convinced of that, and what do you know? So was I!

"So, George. How should we punish Tinisha for saying such errant things about you and I and Krishna? She probably says bad things about Paige and Forest and Sunshiney and you other guys, too, right?" George was taken aback by the very thought of the negative things she had said about us.

"Papa, I want to BITE HER IN THE FACE AND CHEW OFF HER RAMSHACKED MOUTH! That is what I want to do! I want to use my strength to rip her bones from her muscles and to tear her joints from her body! That is what I aim to do... *and that is what I SHALL do!*

"Ok, George. That is a Good Thing. Bring it on, my Lion!"

George liked the thoroughfare. "I shall do it, papa! I SHALL DO IT!"

And that concluded that conversation. We had a talk about science. But that one is private... for now. I shall bring it up later... perhaps.


George began to carry on while Krishna was getting ready to go to work tonight. "Hey papa! Papa! Krishna! I want to go to Guadalcanal! What do you say about THAT?" George was extremely excited!

Krishna spoke up as she was putting work stuff in her carry-on baggage. "Sheesh, George! What are you going to do in Guadalcanal?"

I wanted to tell him that there were terrorists there inside of the country, but he interrupted me and said: "I want to fly a flag there! The Guadalcanal flag and the American flag next to it! What do you say?"

Krishna said: "If you want to fly a flag, go fly on over Iwo Jima! We can get a trip to that island and fly a flag there! And you will..."

I interrupted her with the facts. "I have been to Iwo Jima already when I was on deployment with the Marines. There are statues on the hill on the top of the island that are of American soldiers holding up American flags. There is a statue of the ones in the painting of it in the museums. So, there is no point in wanting to fly a flag there, either. Sorry. There isn't any reason."

"Oh, I didn't know that," Krishna said. "What do you think about that statement, George?" She was wondering if he was going to get irate over the facts.

He didn't. "That is funny that we took over Okinawa during World War Two and put some statues on it. Funny! At least we won the war, right? Right?" George was excitable, and he said again: "Right? I said RIGHT? ANSWER ME!"

"Right George, right! No need to carry on about it!" I was trying to end the conversation, but Krishna took command of that ending.

"I've gotta go. See you two later, you Magnificent Hero and you Elegant Lion! See ya!" Krishna liked us two a lot. She liked the animals too, but she didn't say anything about them because she was on her way out the garage door. I said bye to her and shut the door after she walked past it to the car. Then I locked the door and turned on the alarm. Then I came into my room and typed this part of this document.

And that was that for today!


"Papa? What is a "Piranha"? I don't know what they are!" George was asking questions.

"George, a piranha is a fish that eats people. They come in big groups of piranhas and they sweep over the swimmers and they eat them that-a-ways. That is what they do! Man-eating creatures, they are!" I hoped he got it in his mind that we weren't supposed to swim in waters infected by piranhas.

George got interested... "Papa, we can bring Tinisha to the waters in Africa with the piranhas in it and we can drive her into the water and thus allow for her to be CONSUMED by the rowdy piranhas! Yes! That is how we can get rid of her for her ill-being behavior towards us! Yes! *That is exactly what we should do!*"

"We could do that, George," I said, but included the fact that we ourselves wanted to avoid going in the water because we would get eaten if we went into it. I said it resolutely, as the definition of a concern.

George didn't like it, but he went and understood it. He responded with a question: "Papa... you don't think I do bad things against you, do you? You don't want to throw me among the piranhas like Tinisha, do you?" George was really concerned, and he had a drawling wimp in his voice.

I tried to calm him down. "No, George, you are an Excellent Lion! I don't want you to go get eaten by the piranhas! That is a horrible thought you have! Where did you get that idea from?"

"I got it from you, papa! You kept on saying bad things about me a few days ago and that made me really decompensated! So, it was natural for me to think that you wanted me to get eaten by fish. Do you hate me for thinking that?"

"No, George... I understand. Just so long as you know now that it was in error. You shouldn't have ever thought I wanted you to get eaten. That is horrible!"

"Yeah, papa... it is horrible. I won't do it again."

"That is good, George. Do you have any questions?"

George thought for a moment, then he asked: "Papa, do you hold the eating of Steak against me? I ask because you haven't given me any for a long ass time. I would like some, you know. What is the deal?" George was really sad.

I wanted to cheer him up, and the fact was that me and Krishna had planned already to go to the Steak restaurant tonight to get something to eat. And we were going to surprise George and Peter the Lion by taking them there for Steak and Asparagus. I told him about it, and he got excited.

"I am so pleased to hear that, Papa! Thank you much!"

"Ok, George, no problem. I hope you enjoy your dinner. I know you like steaks, so we are getting you some. What do you say?""Thank you papa! Thank you thank you thank you!"

I could tell that George was excited over getting some steak tonight... and he deserved it! That is what I thought!

I went on got on the computer and began to write on it. I was listening to music on the TV. It was nice music. Well played and sung.

MacGor killed George's grandpa with a shovel. Horrible. Peter the Rabbit pointed it out to me.

"Papa, do you think we should get same fancy put together pearls for mama's birthday? I want to get her some nice ones. She will appreciate them... she WILL she WILL! Can we get her some for her birthday? Can we? I have enough money for it. Dozens of dollars!" George was making up stories, but he was excitable.

"No, George, you don't have enough money for that. And neither do I!" I was resolute in my explanation to him.

"Well, in George's world, no burglar wants pearls or diamonds... they will take BEEF!" George responded in kind. Then he tried to change the story to something better. "Pa pa who's my hero pa, well you are you are!

You are an upcoming hero in outstanding ways! Look at you a'floating on the breeze! Your feet are tall and strong and sound! The limericks of limericks abound! Papa, you are the hero of the kindest word! That is my song to you, papa!"

I wanted to reward him with a compliment: "George, that is an OUTSTANDING song... it IS it IS! Thank you so much for singing it to me!"

George kept on singing because he liked the compliment. This time his had a different paraphernalia. "My uncle was a kangaroo, a kangaroo. Hiipie di hoppy di kangaroo kangaroo. Sing the song, yes you will yes you will! And never shall you get your hovel ill!" That was a good song, except the negative ending of it. But that was okay. The rest of the song was ideal.

Later down the road, George asked me: "I want some vittles! Can you give me some vittles, papa? Can you can you?"

I had to ask him the question: "What kind of vittles do you want, George?"

He responded with glory! "Give me fried chicken, papa! Some of that fried chicken that you had in the box! Give it to me now, won't you?"

I was sad for George, because I had eaten all of that fried chicken and there was none left for him. "I am sorry, George, but I ate it all. I am sorry!" I was very sad for him and confessed my error to him.

"Papa, never mind!" pronounced George. "The real question is this... what do you want for Christmas?" George was still full of glory. I could tell by the nature of his pronunciation. "Tell me tell me tell me!"

"Oh, George, I know I don't want any more clothes. I have enough of those... Let me think about it and I will tell you when I have an answer."

"Ok, papa. Ok."

I carried on: "By the way, George, what do you want me to get you for Christmas?" I was distinctly curious.

Krishna spoke up to George... "Don't tell him anything about that, George! That is a secret! A CAPITAL SECRET! Don't let him know the Secret!" Krishna was really outspoken on the issue.

George responded in kind... "Ok mama! I shall listen to you and tell papa NOTHING!"

"That's it, George. That's it!" announced Krishna.

"That is horrible!" I said, feeling downtrodden. But that was the way it was. I hated it when they kept Secrets from me, because it was a capital Secret and that was of the highest order. And to think that the Lion was made after my intelligence. Why couldn't he share it with me? Because there was something special in the ramifications of doing it, I was sure of it. But there was nothing that I could do to prevent it. So, I didn't even try.

Krishna gave it a moment. I had George laying on the bed of Krishna next to me as I was writing on the computer. She came over and said to George: "Hey George, do you want to have your pillows? They are nice and comfortable for you to lay on! Here you go..." And she picked him up and put the two little pillows down on the bed next to my head and rummaged George over to them and raised up upwards onto the top of them. He liked it and he thanked her.

"My uncle was a kangaroo my aunt was a giraffe! My auntee was a golden doodle golden doodle golden doodle her name is Paige! There is no papa like you! I tell people there is no papa like mine I say I say, he's a hero in my eyes every day I say I say! Yes indeed I say I say!" George picked up the song and began to sing it again out of nowhere. He really liked that song! He rephrased it nicely!

George changed the subject. "Papa," he asked me, "can you ride a donkey?"

I answered him resolutely: "Of course I can ride a donkey! Why do you ask such strange questions?"

"Because if you can't ride on a donkey then you should ride on a donkey! You should get some donkeys to ride when you move to Idaho so that you will have a divine creature under your legs! That is what I think you should do! Did you like the baclava that you were given? My uncle was a kangaroo, a kangaroo, a kangaroo, whoo hooo!" George kept on going on even after he was done with that part.

"I like kangaroos, George! How do you know?"

"Because I am a copy of your mind, papa!" George was

really elegant. "Did you now that Sunshiney the cat keeps on asking me to give you some treats? How does she know that you are hungry? What about when she is sitting on the bed and she wants to move her torso around? Does she only do that when you interrupt her steadfastness with the movement of your foot? Well? What is the story behind *that?*"

"That is the way that cats operate, George. And you are part cat... you know. The Lion part of you is kin of the cat family. Did you know that?" I was trying to be precise with my terminology. I was, too. George got what I was talking about.

"I understand papa. I understand. It is true, too! I just don't pretend to understand what Sunshiney's mind is all-about because she is a home-cat and not a Lion or Tiger!" George was on the defensive position.

I responded kindly. "I understand George. You make a lot of sense."

"Papa! I really like you a lot! You are an excellent man! Praise be on you, my hero! That is what you are! A wartime hero! A Military harbinger of hope and justice! How do you do it so profoundly, mister? How do you do it? It is magical! A Mystery is what it is! A Capital Mystery! A Miracle!" George was excited for me. He was pleased that I operated so profoundly.

I thanked him for the appreciation. "Thank you, George! Thank you! I am so glad that you feel that I am full of magic and capitalized Mysteries and Miracles! That really pleases me a lot!"

"I have a question though, papa. What do you think the readers of this book will think of the conversations we have with each other? Will they like them? Or do you think they will think they are odd, considering that those idiots would think that I am "just a doll" or something stupid like that. I am a LION! I am NOT just a doll! I have intelligence and such things as thought and speech! Dolls don't have that!" George was rambunctious about his statements, because he felt really soundly about the subject matter. George wanted to hear my take on the subject.

I gave it to him. "You are right, George. I feel like a good man. And YOU are an excellent Lion, you are! There is no reason why you should put yourself into the throes of being rambunctiously neglected throughout your existence. That is why I like it that you like to hang around me! I feel a desire to treat you well and to give your brain respect! And that is what I think that people who read over this book should do. They should *like* the way you speak!"

"That is true, papa. I hope they like the way I speak too. That is the speak of a Lion in the mood for plentiful cheer! That is what it is! I hope that they appreciate that and see it the way it is!"

"They will, George... they will. It is my Will that such a thing occurs! And it will!"

"Cheers!" said George, "cheers and goodwill!"

Little did George know that he and I were going to war.

# CHAPTER 7

## ME AND GEORGE THE LION GO TO WAR

I woke up this morning thinking... "What would it be like to go to War with George?" Then I began to wonder... "Where did THAT idea come from?" Then I began to wonder if that effect was going to happen... if I was going to have to go to war with George.

And it did.

This is how it happened...

George then asked me, in a roundabout manner: "Papa, what are your memories of being inside of Force Reconnaissance Company? I have some details of your memories infused into mine, but the verbiage of what actually occurred doesn't make much sense to me. I am a smart Lion, that is true, so I SHOULD get it... but I don't! I can't help but wonder why a ferocious lion doesn't understand the onset of how war works!" George was saying it confused because he didn't understand how his mind was working. There was something in him that wanted me to deliver the details of the operations to him for some reason. I didn't know, yet, that the reason was so he could use it during a time of war against terrorists. But that was to be determined later in my own mind.

"George, there are a lot of details that go into training for and going into and waging war. I know about the first two episodes. Not the third... because I never went into war. But I trained for it a lot for 11 years. And for a few months we went into a terrorist-held area and trained to take them down. I can teach you about the details of such a thing!" I was trying to be absolute with George and to tell him the good news that I would be able to train him in the details... even if I had gotten out of the USMC some 15 years ago. I had memory of the details of it that I kept in my brain. And the memories of how to navigate and do Calling For Fire with Artillery and firing a weapon and hitting a target were universal and easy to remember. So, I was prepared to give George that information in the best mental profligate methods that I could come up with.

"Can I fire a weapon, papa? I have very short arms, and a rifle is big and long! I won't fit! What am I supposed to do?" George was not happy about it.

"We can see if a manufacturer can make a rifle that fits in your arms and fires bullets. He would have to have a Lion's personality or be partly a Lion to do it, to make it the right length to fit in your tiny arms. But it can be done! The only problem is that the bullets might not be big enough to kill a man-sized object." I was thinking deeply about the issue and trying to come up with a solution that works well for George and the man who was with him in combat... me!

"That will work, papa! If the man is as smart as I am and you are, then he or she will be able to manufacture a weapon that is the right size for combat! COMBAT! That is what I need to learn to do! What if a war starts near here? What if we go to China and you bring me with you, and we come across terrorists? What will we do then? We will pull out our pistols or our rifles and we will engage the terrorists with small-arms fire and shoot them TO DEATH! THAT is what we shall do! Yes! I can see it happening already!" George was excitable with saying it. He liked the idea of having a manufacturer make the rifle and pistol so he could use them. He thought that was a magnificent idea!

"So, how would that work that a manufacturer could get the bullet in range if it is so small?" I asked George.

"Because I will move the aspects of my mind to

within range of the bullet in the gun in the casing to drive it outwards with mental power to make it accelerate to be moving at a speed the same as the speed of being near light speed... which is possible... and able to be held within the aspects of matter and energy within the bullet fragments! The core of the bullet shall move extremely fast and into the chest and skull of the Enemy soldiers and troops and KILL THEM! That is what shall happen! And I can do it with my mind! I have the distinct capability of making matter and energy do some amazing things with my mind! Watch me... *I shall show you!*" George was well-spoken and really put his ideas forwards, even though they seemed to defy the onset of science and physics... he still brought them forwards to me. That was so nice of him, and well-spoken you would not believe it. I believed he could do it, too. I believed!

I told him, too. "I believe you, George, I believe you!"

And at that I turned the news on TV and began to watch the TV News Channel that was on. I am not going to say the name of it here, because it is private and I don't want you to look up the channel online and to look up the channels to see if what I am writing here is "Fiction". That would be no good. So, don't do it! And I will give you no means to do it, anyways! So, There!

The news had a story on China. There was a picture of some inhabitants of China running through town next to shops with fish and herbs in them. They were fleeing something. Then the story went over to the inside of a shop, and in there was an orb of might that was flowing energy through the bodies of inhabitants with erroneous faces. They looked like they were being possessed. That is because they were. As the scene progressed, the possessed people became filled full of energy and they perused themselves outside to attack the natural inhabitants of the city area. They were Terrorist Mutants.

Was it real? Was such a thing actually happening, or was it some made-up news? It was real. Everything in the picture seemed like it was a real picture WITHOUT special effects or any of that in it. And as I watched, George got more and more active... panting at first then saying things off the top of his head out loud that made no sense... but they were in relation to what we had just seen on TV.

"Whaddyababba doghnuttomble whereischerd! Zentra vircumbeshund! Whateveishenscha torblenschad!" George's rendition was full of no English words or no English syllables but drew sense in the deepest realms of the mind of me that it made perfect sense. He was talking about the magic behind the onset of the amazing powers of the Terrorist Mutants... and it made perfect sense in it's odd and bizarre way.

George had the mental powers of a superhero! He could understand things regarding science and magic and other species in such a manner that he could develop all kinds of strategies to do things about them. And his rendition of syllables that he spoke in a bizarre and superhuman nature was a portrayal of what we were to do about those Terrorists with our magic warfare powers! All I had to do was transition to George the onset of the capabilities of doing secret and special things that were pervading the atmosphere of doing harm to the Enemy, which in this case was Terrorist Mutants in China! How would we make that happen in a positive light?

I opened with a question: "George, what do you know about the Magic of War? What can you tell me about it with your knowledge of the Force Reconnaissance Company?" I asked him in a calm but resolute tone to let him know that I meant business with his remarks.

"Papa, we don't see things the way that normal people see them. We see things with originality and the origin of miracles! That is why we can see the enemy when we are walking in the woods from a far distance away when they are trying to be hidden. We SEE things! We navigate by reading the map and putting the image of the ground deep within our minds so that we can peruse the drawings and designs of the map with the gesture of walking and seeing the terrain around us... with things from a far-away distance coming up close in our vision so that it seems like it is directly in front of us! That is how we do it! And that goes into shooting, too! Wanna know how?" George was perusing his mental images of the knowledge he just passed to me with the adeptness of a prophet and the know-how of a priest. He really wanted an answer to the question he had just asked me.

"How does the magic affect the mentality of the shooting that occurs in a warzone, George?"

"Because there is an inflow of thoughts that arises from the process of shooting a weapon. You are a person, so you have normal sized arms and a large rifle. Me, on the other hand, I am a tiny Lion... but a Vociferous Creature with a Clamorous Nature... but I have tiny hands and arms! My rifle will be smaller than yours but with mental force I will drive the bullets forwards and at a higher speed than yours, thus driving them through the meat and bones of the enemy to their brains and hearts and thus killing them dead! That is my goal, and so long as we go and get a good-sized gun manufactured for me then such a thing will occur!" George was absolute with his conviction that he was right.

"Yes, George, I can see that you are thinking a lot about the Terrorist Mutants that we saw on the news! Is that what we are to get ready for?"

"Yes it is, papa! Yes it is! The Terrorists shall be on the receiving end of the bullets that we fire at them! Just get me a weapon made for me, will you? Shall I help you decide where to get one made?" George was eager for a Yes.

"I know, George, I know! I shall go to one of the shops by Camp Pendleton in the city by there and I will go in and tell them that I am looking for a gun to be made for a tiny midget soldier that will be sized by your body! That will deceive them into thinking that it is for a small person and not you, a Lion! That will get it done. They will probably want to see the body of the midget before they make it for him... but I will tell them that he likes to keep it private and that I am paying them so they should just make it. That will get them to put real bullets into it and make it go off!"

"That will work, papa! That will work nicely! Then we shall go to China to fight the Terrorists! That is what we shall do, and that is the way it shall go!" George was absolute with his ready speech.

"Sounds like a plan. Let's make it happen!" I said that with the assuredness of a hero. And that was what I thought we would be, fighting the Terrorists in China! So, we took off towards town to make it happen.


I took the bus with George to the Hall-belint Cumberbunds store that provided man-made renditions of military paraphernalia for the soldier to use in combat or training. That was the place with a server inside that took up the arms of giving me and George support in making a rifle that was small enough to fit into George's arms that had a really strong bullet mechanism. The barrel was stitched so that the bullet would be able to rocket through it at a higher speed than usual.

The man who made it was a Genius! He knew about the slopes of the barrel so distinctly and the measurements between the turning of the rounds that he was able to stitch it on there right away. Granted, it took him a couple of hours to stitch it onto such a tiny circumference, but he did, and it was elegant! Matched George's character!

I even pulled George out of his holder for the man to measure George's arms against the handle and the grip of the rifle. The man took my saying... let me call him "Harry" for the sake of the book and your understanding of my sentences... Harry took my saying that the rifle belonged to a man that was a pigmy and disabled and a member of the Special Forces at heart and made the gun to match a Force Recon Marine. He knew it was Force Recon without me even saying anything about it because he was stationed in a city right by Camp Pendleton. Thus, Harry was able to finish the rifle, put in the chamber and the handles, weave them together so that one could be used to generate the ongoing of the bullet out of the chamber, at the right speed and the right circumference, and the right temperature, and THAT was the onset of the rifle that George and I were to use to penetrate the defenses of the Terrorist Mutants in China... as we had seen on the news in an article that was designed for us to peruse!

"Thank you, Harry! Thank you! George is my partner, and we will be going on a Secret mission overseas to fight against Terrorists! And this rifle will do an extraordinary measure towards helping us accomplish that goal!" I was very pleased and wanted Harry to understand that I really appreciated his effort. And I was also getting ideas sent forwards by George who was also telling me a semblance of what to say to Harry. So, I did, and he loved it!

"That is the least I can do for a disabled client. A midget! I never knew that a midget would be accepted into Special Forces! Imagine that it is! I can tell you are telling the truth, but the arms and the nature of the Lion Doll that you brought in here for me to use as the length of the arms of the disabled veteran!" Harry was happy, and so was George. George didn't speak up or say anything out of his own shell to Harry. George didn't want him to know that he was just a Lion... not a Doll!

Me and George left at that and went to the bus stop and waited for a bus. After a very short spell one arrived, and the timing made it seem like the busses schedule was reminiscent of the mindset of the warriors that we were fighting next to in order to get justice in China. That was our goal, and that was the next step... transportation to China by boat!

I took George to the pier in San Diego where the ships debarked to sea. We went up to the boat and there was no line in the way, and we walked along the walkway to the opener and logged in. I kept George in my binder holder so that people couldn't see him. There was a gap on the side of the binder holder that he could see out of and he told me what he saw by using my own voice. Thus, if I seemed like I was talking to myself I was. I thought about it and it seemed like the illusion that I was "mentally ill" ... but it was actually George speaking. That got us by into the boat!

We walked next to the pool and George saw a set of couches next to the pool that were designed for ship-goers to lay on. At that, George said to me: "Hey papa! Do you want to sit out here and do our reconnoitering of the Terrorist Mutants? Do you think that is applicable? Do you? Huh? Huh? Do you?" George was excited about being on the mission with me, and he wanted to discuss everything we could about the warfare we were to become engaged in.

"Sure, George, I'd like to come out her to do the mission! Now, let us get to the room so we can discuss it without you having to go through my head to talk about it! I would like it if you sat down across from me on the table or the bed and we could discuss it like regular people can!" I was precise with that statement and tried to make it as lenient as I could so George wouldn't get offended by the statement. And I think it worked!

"Okay, papa... to the room it is!"

We finally got there, and I sat on the bed. George came out of the knapsack and got put on the bed, next to me. "Thanks papa! That is so nice of you! I have some things that I have been waiting until we were here to tell you... but you might be offended. Wait... you are like ME! So, no, you will NOT be offended! Wanna hear what the things I was thinking were?"

I was extremely curious, because there were a lot of things one could think about going to war. So, I asked him: "What was going through your mind, George?" I was adept at my verbiage!

"Papa, I was thinking... what part of China are we going to go to? This boat goes to Macau and Hong Kong and Shanghai. I think we should get off in Macau. That was born of a Goddess doing good things for the port, and it could be taken over by the Terrorist Mutants! That is where I think we should go! And it has the 4th lowest death rate in the world... so the bad guys would want to do something against it to cause more people to die there! It is good verses the evil of the Terrorists! And even more...!"

"What's that, George? What's more than THAT?"

"There could even be Terrorist Mutants that have infiltrated THIS SHIP before we left harbor and they could be onboard RIGHT NOW! We are going to have to take diligent action to prevent them from mutating us into fallen comrades and such! Horrible! But I am certain they are here... with us! I SAW THEM PAPA STEALING GOODS FROM THE PASSENGERS AND I DIDN'T SAY ANYTHING TO YOU BECAUSE I DIDN'T WANT THEM TO HEAR IT!" George was really loudly spoken now in the room. He was trying to keep us safe from him being overheard by the Terrorist Mutants on board.

So, I answered him in-kind: "George, we shall go ashore in Macau. I think you have a really solid cause for that being the location of the main body of Terrorist

Mutants. We shall go ashore and check it out. And until we get there we shall walk across the board of this vessel and get a full symbiosis of what is going on with the crew. I think you are right... it makes sense that the Terrorist Mutants would go on board a ship to interview and put in arms against the people who would be going overseas to put a stop to them. They are horrible and ossiferous people! That is, if they are even still considered to be people!"

George took what I said at heart. Then he asked me to go over some of what he had become wise about in-regards-to the onset of the doctrine of the Force Reconnaissance Company. Their strategies and such. To that question I replied to him: "There was a lot of thinking that went into mission planning and execution of the mindset of warfare, my friend. There were details that went into navigation over terrain we had never been on, with knowing the locations of the enemy and of calling for fire with artillery or naval guns on them, calling for fire from aircraft was the other main supporting one. And there was the list of immediate action drills we were to do if the enemy ever saw us and engaged us with firearms or rockets. We had to be prepared for all of it... and..."

"Papa, I know about the details of all those aspects because I could read your mind! But you should go over the details of them with me so that we can incorporate them in our actions against the Terrorists in a real-time premise... in part because what I may have gotten from your memory could be wrong or interpreted incorrectly!

I wouldn't like that much, no I wouldn't! But if we look into the makings of the theories then we can identify what works and what doesn't with the technology now at hand. What do you say, papa?" George was flagrant with his intelligent thoughts going on. And he was right! I will say that for sure... he made perfect sense with what he was saying!

"George, I hear you. What should we start with?" I asked him.

"Start with the immediate action drills. You have never been called to fight against a Mutant, have you? Well, that being the focus of our expedition, we are going to need a way to combat them when we run into them. And because I think that there are Terrorist Mutants on board this ship right now, I think we should develop a means to combat them with my new rifle *before we even go outside to meet them!* Can we put together an Action Plan for Combat with them... considering the special characteristics of a Mutant and what they mean towards us... and what they mean towards trying to turn other humans against us?" There was a lot more detail into what George wanted to say but he also wanted me to respond to he could get a full summary of my ideals behind his concepts at hand.

"Well then," I responded, "we are going to have to do a reconnaissance of the Mutants before we engage an immediate action plan so we can get a head's up of what they are all about. So, let us begin a reconnaissance plan first!" I wasn't really sure about that, but it seemed like

it was hard to determine how one would fight against an
enemy that they don't even know about. And the term
"Mutant" determined some skills or powers or states
of being that were different than the regular person's
existence. We needed to tell the difference.

"That is an interesting topic," said George. "What do
we do to determine what an enemy is all about, anyways?
I know some of them from my reconnaissance of your
mind... We must determine what their location is by
using mapping devices and putting the grids of unseen
events, or seen events, involving mutants down on it so
we can read the grid and terrain on the map. We can
use satellite images of mutants doing negative things like
moving weapons of people around on the earth and use
the radio mapping frequency to map it out. We can hook
the computer to the radio and download the signals sent
by the mutants to the real world and decipher what they
say and determine whether they were sent by mutants or
someone related to them or someone else. That is all stuff
that we can do with a computer and a radio. And the news!
The news did that show on the Terrorist Mutants, so they
have footage of the event that came from somewhere on
their file computer or in their office! We can get that
data from the news organizations! So, that is how we can
determine where the mutants are located. Now all we need
to do is find a way to get there without contacting the
mutants and getting done away with. Think of the name
of the enemy, anyways... Terrorist Mutants. That means
that they are seeking out ways to use physics and trauma

to do away with us and to bring us pain or even down to death! Something we must watch out for... let me tell you!" George stopped talking and let me digest the details of what he had said to me. There was a lot involved with mapping the enemy and going to the news organizations and getting details about it. I wondered... perhaps we could go to the mutant arena and film them like we did film the enemy in the Force Reconnaissance Company repeatedly! That would work if we put it together.

I decided to tell George that we should attempt to film the enemy troops and broadcast the data over the radio channels to the rear. Granted, there was no way the radios would handle that much data when I was in the Marines from 1990 to 2005, but that was 15 years ago and that it ended, and technology has come along since then. I mean, look at the capabilities of the average laptop computer nowadays. They have such a high speed and the memory data has changed to smaller discs and they hold a lot of data on the USB discs. Almost a whole computer's memory amount of data! That is my guess, anyways. So, it makes sense that there would be enough comings-along to send images gotten by camera on a computer through space to satellites and have the images sent through to the read areas on the other side of the planet. That is something that must indeed be possible! I told that to George in a group of sentences similar to what I have written down here, and he responded to me.

"Hey papa, that is good and all and you brought your computer, right? That computer had Wi-Fi! It can link into the military servers and get data from them! Do you know the website to the Marines? The Secret one? Call a recruiter and let him know about our mission and GET IT! DO IT NOW! That way we will be able to download the military files on the Terrorist Mutants... because I am sure they have some files on it... and that ways we can get a head's up on the data involved and know about them the same thing that the Headshed of the military knows about them! That will be good and helpful to us, won't it?" George thought that us filming the Mutants or photographing them and sending he data over the radio was the only way to go about it for us. After all, we were just two people. In fact, we were... a handicapped person and a doll Lion. What could we really do?

A lot!

We took a break from speaking and considered how we were going to make the call to the recruiters. Then I did and got the Marine Corps Force Recon website that was Secret. I am not going to put it down here, because it is not to be released to the public. But the recruiter on the other end of the line looked up my name and got my Physical Fitness record from the USMC that described how I had served time in Force Recon Company. And he liked my mission. He thought that was something a veteran would do. He even asked me if I wanted other veterans involved in the mission. I told him "No, that's ok. I'll let you know later. I'm handicapped". So, he said that was okay and gave me the website anyways. Actually, I didn't want to have to explain George to another veteran. They would think I was crazy.

So, from the room I decided that we had to get on a secret server with the Wi-Fi and couldn't do it from the room at that time, because the signal was interrupted by the waves of the ocean. Me and George then decided to go outside by the pool with the computer with George in the knapsack and looking out of the seeing device on the side. I would station it so that he could see out of it and look at my ongoing data exchange on the secret website of the USMC Force Recon.

Me and George in my knapsack took the computer down the walkway and went out the door to the pool area. We didn't run into anyone, but out there by the pool there were people standing by the recliners and moving like they were interested in something. I paid attention to them, wondering if they were Mutants.

We went out and found a recliner off by itself next to a table for the computer. I figured I could keep the computer on my lap and do it that ways but George wouldn't be able to see it accurately that ways, so I put it on the table. We sat down and turned the computer on and looked at the screen. It was illuminated. I put in the password to the computer and the website to the secret Force Recon file website and went in there.

The Force Recon site had a webpage that led to one that had the secret locations of the Terrorist Mutant campaign, and in it was a link to read about what the Mutants were all about. We went to it.

George sat in his bag and looked at the computer screen through the felt window in the corner, looking intently. He looked at the screen and saw there a picture of the terrain of Macau, China next to the mountains there. It was a hovel or a compound of built limestone that was overlooking another couple of buildings that had restaurant paraphernalia attached to the front of it on the street. There were windows on the limestone building and two large doors in the front that looked like they were locked. The question arose in George's mind as he looked at the building of this: "What is inside that building?" The idea came in a mental profusion of ideas stemming from the structure of the building taking up the energy of the thoughts of those moving outside the building or into it or out of it... a frequency of thought that was divine in its interpretive abilities.

What did those thoughts say to George? He was getting ideas of destroying a large semblance of the population in America and the allies of America, because the THINGS within the compound were Terrorist Mutants that hated America! And how did George know they were mutants? Because he got in his head thoughts of thinking odd things about the onset of power within the electrical energy of the planet, and the capabilities of it enabled the mutants to generate a force of thought throughout the field that made the person on the receiving end gestate their cells into mutants themselves and thus convert to mutants without a will of their own. And the mutants would use that power, if the person didn't want to convert and changed their mindset, then the mutants would put in there the power to make their cells break down with fraudulent energy and destroy the brain matter within. Horrible! And George was getting examples of that occurring at the compound among the tourist visitors of it that were normal Americans or Europeans.

I looked at the website of the Terrorist Mutants too, and my interpretation was slightly different than George's. There was within the screen pictures that showed illumination of the windows of the limestone compound. If one looked really close one could see that the picture was moving in real time... there had been a camera put in there by the Force Recon Marines and it was playing film data...and as it showed the shadows over the windows one could see a large linear figure within moving throughout, looking out the window and making bizarre and angry faces. It wasn't really clear because there was a blur on the camera. But it came in a way that an outsider could see it.

And below that picture of the compound window was an explanation in words of the fact that the picture was of an alien lifeform that was hating the Americans and the Europeans and wanting to forwards their destruction by any means necessary. And he was training those Mutant Terrorists within the compound to come out and present arms within the population with mental power within the USA and Europe. Terrible! But it was seen as a real world threat to the Americans, and a threat they would have to endure at every location they went to outside the USA when the terrorists were not within the USA... and within the USA when the terrorists gained the courage to enter the USA on their terrorist mission.

"I wonder if they are coming on this ship," I said quietly to George. I didn't want some Terrorist Mutant supporter to hear what I said, so I said it too quiet for them to hear.

"Papa, see, I TOLD YOU that they were on this ship!" George was more outspoken but still quiet. He waved his arm out of the knapsack and pointed at the pool. Within the pool was a group of 4 men and a woman... all standing there oddly and looking at me from a distance. They were quietly talking about something that they were trying to hide from me reading from their mouths with their hands covering them.

I was convinced that they were Mutant Terrorists, and that they had somehow gotten word from the computer that we were looking at a website about them. That put us at risk of capture and torture.

So, I downloaded my "Erase" program and removed all data from the Force Recon website. Then I turned the computer off and put it back in the backpack. George told me that I needed to go talk to those Terrorists and find out what they were all about. I was concerned that they would follow me to my room and assault me and George there. Now, George had his rifle on him, granted, and I had my pistol in the knapsack next to George in a place where I could get to it readily... but I really didn't want to use it on the ship. We would get in trouble if the pistol went off and the crew, human or not, would come after us. And there was nowhere to hide on a Cruise Ship. Not really. Everywhere had access by the crew. Even downstairs below the deck.

Me and George got up from the recliner and walked in a normal fashion right next to the pool to the door in a straight line towards my room. As I passed the people who were definitely looking like Terrorist Mutants I was walking quickly past them. They immediately started to move to the side towards me and walk out of the pool. I walked in the door and looked behind me. They were walking towards me without drying off. So, I hurried down the hallway, running when I got out of sight of the door to the outside, and went and unlocked my room and immediately went inside of it.

I locked the door from the inside and stood there next to it, listening to the sound of the hallway. I heard those people who I was sure now who were Terrorist Mutants were making noise moving down the hallway, looking for me. They missed the room and went past it. When the space calmed down I went back into the room and lay on the bed. I took George out of his knapsack and lay him down next to me.

George then explained to me what his thoughts on the Terrorist Mutants was from that online video and his mindset of the mental powers of the evildoers. "How do you think we should fight that mindpower, papa? How are we to prevent them from giving us odd ideas that are out of frequency with reality? How do we prevent that?" George was really concerned, because he had had some horrible images of the Terrorist Mutants mindpower in action.

"George, a person… or a Lion… gets a feeling for the different frequencies of thoughts that is either generated by their own head… or PUT THERE by another being! A person can sense the difference! Thus, just go around the Terrorist Mutants and they will begin to promote their errors to you, and you can sense it and tell the difference between their thoughts and yours. Thus, you can DEFINITELY avoid becoming manifested into becoming a Terrorist Mutant! Believe me… it is avoidable! That is why they have the mental power to make your cells interact if you don't become a Terrorist Mutant! But thoughts prevail, my friend. Thoughts prevail. That is why a person can sense when they are trying to modify the cells and think of positive things like them being in a solid structure that prevents the cells from falling apart. That is the power of the mind!" That explained the situation to George. I liked to talk to him about it, because it made my brain work in the nefarious conditions of the being that was entailed by the Terrorist Mutants… at least the possible negative outcomes. They weren't definite, though…my mind had determined that.

We thus transitioned the conversation to another element of the Warfare we were involved in. "George, you read my mind when you were being created. What do you know about Calling for Fire with Artillery or Naval Gunfire against the enemy troops?" I wanted to ask him to determine if there was anything that I should tell him before we came into further contact with the Terrorist Mutants. I wanted to have a way to strike them from the ship, if that is what needed to happen. I figured that Artillery Gunfire would do the trick. And there were Naval Gunships within reach of us where we were on the Pacific Ocean. We were within range of Hawaii. There were all sorts of heaps of Naval Vehicles there. I knew this because we had gone there and seen them when I was in Force Recon Company.

George answered me resolutely. "They know the range and the speed of the firearms in relation to the grid line that you give them to fire to. They have a global recognition system that allows them to fire on any land that had had satellite grid sensing involved in it to determine the actual grid that we give them over the radio. And it takes a lot of energy and effort to deviate from the grid sense that the USA military has in its hands. So, we have the grid sensing system within your head. You have learned it from the radios that they have given you in Force Recon Co. and that plays a big part into finding the actual grid because of the program on the radio that enables you to do it wholesale. That is my call. Let us do it now! Let's go find those Terrorist Mutants and call for fire on them from the Navel Gunships and destroy them wholesale! That is my call papa! Take it or take it!" George was speaking with the fury and anger of a commander just outside the range of bringing fire on the enemy. And that was what we were. Within range of them. All we needed to do was to go out by the pool or into the gym with the radio or the computer and to progress to call fire on and destroy the enemy troops. But there was a problem.

"What do you think that the crew of the ship will think if some unknown Terrorists got shot down on ship. The crew probably doesn't know that they are terrorists! They will see who is on their computer and bring in the artillery against US!" I was concerned about that. I knew that was the way the boat would operate.

George had an answer. He always did. "Papa. We can hide that we are on the computer when we do it. Or we can go there, see the Terrorists, because they don't move much, they keep on waiting for someone to assault, and we can come over to the room them and get on the computer without being present. What do you say?"

I thought for a moment. Then I answered him. "I think the first one will work better. We don't want to call fire from this room without being there to see the fire coming in. Because what would happen if we left and some aggressors came in and the Terrorists went after them the way they went after us before and we couldn't then shoot them because we couldn't see them? I think it is better just to keep our computer usage secret. Besides... when they get blown up they won't be able to call for support against us, will they?" That answered THAT, I thought.

"Ok, papa... let's do it!" George was excited for the action. I was pleased. I liked it when the Lion was active and communicable with me. He liked my idea, and that pleased me. He was such an active Lion. And a hallmark of Warfare! He was ready to get into the action therein. So, we went outside with the computer, with the website of the Naval Guns already entailed within the computer for us to transcribe the grid to. Now, granted, it was hard to determine exactly what our grid was because we were out in the ocean. But with a search I found that there was a readily available website to the navigation system of the cruise liner we were on, and therein were numbers reflecting our actual gridline based on the geography of the ocean. That was enough for a Naval vessel to fire on us with the awe and precision of an excellent rifle expert. An expert! That is what we needed!

We sat on the bench with the computer out and George within the knapsack and listened for the fire to overwhelm our ship. We looked out at sea and couldn't see a ship but suddenly saw some glimmer of gasses erupting from a cannon over the horizon's edge. We looked at the Terrorist Mutants in the pool and wondered what they would do when they saw the glimmer. They paused in their action, then suddenly two missiles burst over the top of the ship downwards and catapulted onto their bad location. They erupted in fire and gas and blew the pool apart. The alarm on the ship started to go off, and eventually maintenance men came through the door to the pool with containers of gas-retardation devices and they blew it on the fire to put it out. The bodies of the Terrorist Mutants were blown up and rifled with scabs from the intense heat that killed them off.

I was so happy! We had won! The question I had was this: What are the remaining Terrorist Mutants going to do now? Will they try to invade the ship that shot at us? What is the ship's crew going to do now that we were hit by Naval Gunfire and they didn't know why? Did they know why? I didn't know, but I figured that me and George were going to find out soon.

We went back into the room while the alarm went off. The people around the pool had fled when the blasts went off and didn't come back for a long time. In the meantime, we were sure that the crew of the ship was calling on their radios as many frequencies as they could in an attempt to find out who was on the other line that had bombed the ship for what seemed like no reason... and it had killed about six people. Six. That is the number of lies. Me and George knew the number because they announced it over the radio. As a whole, the radio had stopped playing music before we got back to the room because the crew had silenced it and replaced it with their emergency signal and emergency communications after the blast. They had announced on their frequency the number of people who were killed at the pool, and they didn't even say anything about them suspecting that the fools killed were Terrorist

Mutants. Nope. They said nothing about that. The way they put it, it sounded like they were innocent victims. A complete mistake. Maybe even a lie. I imagined that there were some Terrorist Mutants that had infected the staff for control of the ship. And there were no staff members killed in the blasts. So, the Terrorist Mutants were not completely defeated.

But George and I had shown that we had a degree of capability in the calling for fire among the Naval Gunships. So, we did well at that regards. George was doing really well at becoming a solid warrior. I wondered... how does he shoot? Is he really accurate the way that I was in the USMC? He should be since he has my mental powers. And the guy in the town we went to at the Reserves Store made George a divine looking weapon that is the right size for his little bitty paws to work on. He liked the weapon, and so did I. The question was... How will he shoot with it?

That was the next question for us to find out. We persuaded each other to do some more on the Terrorist Mutants. We agreed to go a'shooting at the bad guys within the staff of the ship.

So, we first took a nap and let them get organized. Then we went a'huntin'.

We departed the room and went down the stairs to the lower deck. George had his firearm at the ready within his paws and was stationed within the knapsack, ready to jump up along the top of the svelte covering to the bag and to fire as ready on the perpetrator mutant. He was ready to go! I thus walked down the steps to the ladder well that ran to the below portions of the ship. The door was locked with a code console on the front of it. But I wanted to get in! I didn't know what code to put on there, and I thought that we could go back upstairs to the pool deck and see what the people up there had written down, in an effort to get the code. But then a man came downstairs and walked up to the door that we were standing next to. He walked right by us and said nothing.

Then he displayed impatience and went to the door and punched in the code. It was a 4 letter code, like others around the city on the iPhones, and the door opened. I was watching him put the code in, so I thereby got a semblance of what the code consisted of. The door opened, and the man looked over at me and saw me looking at the code as he put it in. He immediately got agitated, and it was clear from his behavior that he was a mutant terrorist.

In a reaction to seeing me see him put the code in he immediately began to send mentally to my mind signals of mental distress. He was trying to drive me crazy so the staff could put me in detention and take away my ability to go below. I could sense the errant thoughts. So could George. But George had a failsafe to mental trauma installed in his genes, so he projected to me a solution to the problem. My mind cleared up with a sense about it that there were errant thoughts that were not mine involved in the repercussion of ideas I was having. Thus, I was able to do-away with the errors. And at the same time George reacted...

George pushed up on the svelte covering and opened himself a way out. It was an immediate reaction. As he did it he pushed himself upwards on his legs to the top of the knapsack and pointed the small rifle at the mutant terrorist trying to mindtrip us. George pointed the rifle at the man and aimed it and pulled the trigger. A bolt of electrical energy came smashing out of the barrel of the gun, launching a tiny bullet full range across the walkway to the neck of the terrorist mutant. The bullet went through the middle of his neck and splattered out the opposite end against the doorway... which was opening now. The terrorist mutant went down dead, and the door opened up for us to go through.

I was very pleased. It was apparent that the weapon that I had given to George was working with divine capabilities. I was happy that was the case. George was happy as well. He raised his rifle upwards with both paws and cheered himself. "We did it, papa! We killed the Terrorist Mutant! Let us go a'huntin' even further into the realm of the bad guys and see how many we can kill! I have plenty of ammunition! Let us give it a try!" George was excited. He really wanted to kill many of those bad guys and gals. I say "gals" too because when we were by the pool with the computer and seeing the Terrorist Mutants up there, there were sets of female Terrorist

Mutants present. There was both sexes among those who sought to do ill to the rest of us passengers.

And it seemed like the place where the ship was attempting to take us was to China. Why China? Because most of the Terrorist Mutants that me and George had seen had been Chinese in descent. It seems that there was something there within that country where the Terrorist Mutants were coming into fruition among the people and occupying their space with their negative characters. No wonder why they wouldn't make a decent Trade Deal with us!

Me and George walked down the walkway past the now unlocked door. We were hoping that the code to get outside the door was the same as the one to get inside of it from the outside. But we couldn't try it out because we were worried that there would be a detection mechanism within the door that would tell the bad people that we had put the same code in twice in a near-time zone. Nope. Couldn't risk that. So, we trusted that it was the same for simplicity purposes, and we walked down the walkway, looking for the Control Panel room where we imagined that there would be a lot of Terrorist Mutants.

We came down the hallway to a control room. Within it were supply members who were all sitting at tables that were against computer screens with illustrations on them. They were gazing up at it, not moving, except their hands were jittering. George and I looked soundly at them, and their eyes, and saw within their glasses were illuminated beams of light that was black. They had the eyes of the dead. The screens had a picture of the people on board the ship, within the common areas. Within that area were also pictures of people who were Terrorist Mutants glowing in a colored black orb. Thus, the Terrorist Mutants were marked, but there were not that many of them around. Most of them had been destroyed in the blast of energy from the other warship. The remainder of the Terrorist Mutants were reacting to it, trying to find a way to assert control of the inhabitants of the ship without letting their presence being known.

The outcome was clear. There were about 15 different Terrorist Mutants in the area. But they were blind with dead eyes that saw nothing but what was on their computer screens. Thus, it was clear that we would be able to shoot and kill many of them before the others would be able to respond to our warfare. And they deserved it. They were trying to use their powers to do all sorts of negative things to good passengers who were innocent and had done nothing to them. They disagreed with the thoroughfare of the passengers and wanted to defeat them with an arduous force of evil thought-experiments. And they wanted to keep the warfare secret. Cowards! Thus, it was apparent what me and George needed to do. We needed to close into a position that put us within range of just one or two of the Mutants, but that was quiet and secret to the other Mutants.

We found a spot to get started. There was one Terrorist Mutant of dead-looking appearance sitting at a desk near the entrance on the walkway, and he was across the hall from another desk that was separated from the other desks by a wall of grey paint. There was no way for the others to know that their buddies were being shot, unless they could hear the bullets being released from the barrel... which they certainly could. But they were dead-looking, so, would they react? I didn't think so, but George wasn't sure. George thought there COULD be a chance that they would react. But they wouldn't know the exact location of the bullets, right? So, it would take some time for them to react against me and George. Or so we thought.

It didn't matter, then. George already had his rifle out and he raised up the knapsack and rapidly fired shots at both of the Terrorist Mutants sitting down. They both, dead, immediately jerked their arms upwards and fell down on the floor. Now they were truly dead. We looked over at the other ones, the remaining 13 of them for a view of their reaction, and there was none. The gun George had used had made the shooting noise, true, but the Terrorist Mutants were not reacting to it. They were too close to being dead with their attention fixated on the computer screens at their forefront. Stupid fools. They had no understanding of what was about to happen to them.

George and I stepped into the labyrinth and walked to another secret spot. There were three Terrorist Mutants available there. Two were sitting next to each other and one was across the way. George aimed and opened fire on all three of them, one right after the next after the next.

He shot them all in the prescribed location... the neck. It was already proven that bullets to the neck of Terrorist Mutants would interrupt their airflow and disrupt their existence by bringing them quickly to death. And it only took one bullet per Terrorist Mutant to do the trick. That was a distinct weakness among the creatures. And George and I took advantage of it readily. All three of the Terrorist Mutants were dead.

That left ten of them remaining.

We planned on killing them forthwith. But first, George checked his ammunition and saw that he had only used about 5 rounds out of the 60 that he had been carrying. George wanted to make sure that he had extra ammunition besides the one shot amounts that he was using to kill the Terrorist Mutants, so that he would have some ammunition to use in the rare event that something could go wrong with the shooting and he would need the extra rounds to shoot down the Terrorist Mutants altogether.

George counted that he had enough rounds for about five rounds per target, with a few extras. He figured that would be enough to kill the remaining ten of them.

We crept up to a space with another five of them in it. There were three sitting at a long counter staring at the computer screens, and two more sitting opposite of them. They were divided from the others by a tall computer screen that went from the ceiling to the floor. There were pictures of the common areas on it, and a large picture of Washington DC on it. The Capital of the USA was it. The Terrorist Mutants were planning on taking out the Capital of the USA! Horrible! That prepared us more than anything. We were definitely going to take them out.

George was already leaning outside of the knapsack with his rifle, and as soon as we moved within range he pointed and began to fire his weapon. One shot, two shots, three shots, four shots, then a noise from the rifle. He was out of bullets in that magazine! Quickly he reloaded his magazine, and saw, with his eyes, that the remaining Terrorist Mutant that hadn't been shot had sensed that the others were dying. The Terrorist Mutant began to move around with his head and look around at the two of us pointing the weapon at him! He started to make a moaning noise in alarm! He was grunting out loud! He suddenly began to draw the attention of the other remaining five!

George saw the comings-on of the Terrorist Mutants and reloaded his magazine quickly. Then he fired! Quickly, he shot and killed the first one. Then we ran down the hallway to the opening area of the laboratory with the screens of the computer equipment shifting vision to look through monitors at the area that we were in. The Terrorist Mutants were all in glowing black spheres and me and George were lit in colors. The Terrorist Mutants were looking at the picture then the room to ascertain what was going on there.

George and I took no part in it besides to draw ourselves into their area and to begin to fire upon them all! Bang! Bang! Bang! Bang! That paid them reminiscence of the gunfire we had presented against them! We shot one of them, then two of them. The remaining three heard the gunshots and turned in their seats and started to bolt after us. As they got closer George took careful aim and fired again! Bang! Another one dead! Then there were two left.

They came bolting at the same time and arrived at our bodies at almost the same time. George fired on one hastily and missed his neck. He hit him in the bottom of the collar and it didn't kill him. Then he fired the second one and it hit the guy's neck, and he pummeled flat and lay down dead. The last one didn't hesitate. It came in and it swatted at George, not even noticing that he was a Lion! George fired his rifle at the same time as getting swatted, and the bullet fell down to the lower portions of the Terrorist Mutant. George realized that he was in danger, so he moved the rifle upright immediately and began to fire at the Terrorist Mutants chest multiple rounds. There were three rounds left. Then George saw that the Terrorist Mutant was stumbling around but not dying, so George quickly reloaded his magazine with three more bullets and with careful aim fired all three rounds at the Terrorist Mutant's neck!

Thus, the Terrorist Mutant was killed dead. And George had only faced a swat. He wasn't damaged. Just his paw hurt, along with his arm. He had gotten swatted sidebar. But he was okay.

George and I decided that we were not going to go after any more of the Terrorist Mutants after that. We didn't have enough ammunition. So, we went back to our room.

We were so happy with our success that we wanted to celebrate. There was tea in the refrigerator and juice as well, and we were thirsty from all the hard work we had done. So, being fruitful, I pulled a jug of juice from the fridge and poured it into a glass and gave the glass to George to drink. He gobbled it up delightfully! He was so happy and insatiable! He had a glass and he wanted more! I fulfilled his desires!

And with that, the war against Terrorist Mutants continued, but that is a story in and of its own. I have made it clear that the Terrorist Mutants could be destroyed by Naval Gunfire, Aircraft Artillery, and rifle fire. It is an excellent chapter. But that is all there is to say about it right now. More may be said later. I am keeping open the options of writing more into that story. But I am sure that people probably won't be wanting to read it. So, I probably won't write any more on the subject. But what I have written so far is really nice! And it is about the behaviors of the Excellent Lion named George!

# CHAPTER 8

## ANOTHER CHAPTER ON PETER AND PETER AND PEACHES AND PERLE

This is the last Chapter on those remarkable animals. It is going to go into their ability to create Magic!

There is a Lion, a Rabbit, and two Unicorns. Imagine the magical powers that they must have! Hwood and Disney and book publishers have made movies and books about the stories of the Lion, the Rabbit, and the Unicorn. They have been remarkable stories. And they lead up to me writing this story and trying to stimulate the same effectiveness within my story as those stories had. I am doing it with my own Creativity and Endurance. I am writing a lot in this story. And I am putting my imagination to a high effort to imagine and memorize as much detail as I can so that I can write about it all within this remarkable novel!

With that said, let me introduce the introduction to Krishna about the subject matter I want to cover. I want to enable her to give me solid input on the speeches and ideas of the animals so that I can put it down on paper and make my computer put it to life!

So, HERE GOES!

I asked Krishna today to tell me about the Magic those four do. Krishna replied: "What are you talking about? Peter the Lion and Peter the Rabbit have no magical powers! They are just animals! But the Unicorns... Peaches and Perle...well, that is a different story. They ARE Unicorns after all! They have the magical powers of being so!" Krishna was full of adulation.

"So, what would the Unicorns do that is magic?" I asked her.

"They would read the minds of the recipients and if they were good people then the Unicorns would do Good Things for them. It would be based on their thought-streams." Krishna already knew the answer to that question and was waiting for me to ask it with the answer already within her mind. So convenient of her to do!

I responded to her statement: "That is so good of us to know! Good with a capital "G"! I mean it! Stop making it out to be a horror movie, what I just said! It is POSITIVE!" I was saying that last statement to the reader just in case they were for some nefarious reason saying crazy things about what I had written for them.

Krishna gave her response to that: "That is a good thing for you to say. It gives the term "Good" enough credence!"

"Thank you, Krishna!"

"You're welcome. Now, let us talk about what elements of Magic will be like to the receiver of it!" Krishna was ready to carry the conversation onto the subject matter of the meaning of the discussion.

"Talk about the elements of magic?" George interjected, "Whatever do you mean? You two would have to say what is on your minds first to make that happen!" George didn't understand that he didn't have the capability of doing magical behavior, I didn't think. He wanted to know what was on me and Krishna' minds.

Krishna started out... "Well, for starters, I am wanting to start to do a Yoga program and get this big fat weight off of my body. I weighed myself the other day and had gained 15 pounds! That is evidence of eating too many carbohydrates and sugars over Thanksgiving and Christmas! I am getting fat and have to do something about it!"

She was standing next to the stove when she was talking with her back to me. I could see her butt. It was big. "Krishna, your butt is really big. That is where the weight went. You need to do some sit-ups or something like that to do away with the big ass you have."

"Yeah, my butt is really big. I need to fix that!" said Krishna.

"You should do the Yoga exercises and wave your hand over your head and take in the steak!" said George. "Then wave your other hand around with the Yoga and draw in Lamb Chops! Yes! That would be so nice! The diet will help you lose weight... it will it will!" George was excited with his speech. He was hungry too! He loved to talk about food. It made him feel wholesome.

The real question was this: what elements of Magic were the Unicorns thinking of doing for the conversations that we people and George had just had?

I came out and spoke for Peaches the Unicorn. "Peaches has sent me a mental image! She said that there is going to be a YouTube video that is attached to the iPhone Krishna has that will be instructions on how to Perform Yoga. The instructions were excellent! They were put together by the genius of Peaches! She put them in video and enabled the transfers to the iPhone with clear data and she even made the screen clear and precise! She even prepared it within the memory!" It was an excellent experience. I really had a lot of respect for Peaches and Perle.

Krishna then said: "So what is the network that the Unicorns are using for us? Is it YouTube?" Krishna then pulled her iPhone out and looked at her message button.

Sure enough, she had a new email from the YouTube account that was to a video of yoga students doing the exercises and moving their bodies around. "Oh, look! I've got it! So nice of those Unicorns to do! And the video and criteria of statements put forth on the video over the bodies of the exercisers is remarkable! There was a lot of thought that went into it! Was that the Unicorns that did that? How can their minds operate so profoundly?"

"I don't know, Krishna. But I do know that the Unicorns are really smart. They have mental images of people that join in fact with comprehension of their abilities and actions! That is what I have seen in them. But their Magic... man... that was kept Secret until today!" I was solid in my speech. Krishna liked it.

Krishna asked me the following question: "So, what other ideas have the Unicorns sent to your direction? Have they said that they are doing any other Magic for us... something besides Yoga? What is the Yoga all about, anyways?"

"The Yoga is about getting elements and particles of your body to do things that are miraculous that allow for you to do things that the average body wouldn't be able to do in the average time. Things like heal from injuries. Yoga will make you healthier by preventing disease. It will also make you healthier in general by making you stronger and increasing your immunity systems. That is so righteous! It is a Holy exercise. It is one that allows for one to think of the religious aspects of existence as they go though the process of the Yoga. And there is more to the message than that…" I continued, "The physical fitness of the recipient plays a big part in it. The Unicorns shall be bringing forwards Good Health to Krishna. In between, they will be bringing Good Health to me! So, it is clear to me that the Unicorns are well thought out and are doing things with an aura of excellence!" I felt well spoken.

"It is good that they will be taking care of your health, papa! But what about mine? Will they be taking care of me? I want to be cared for… I do I do! Will they care for me… will they?" George was highly emotional over the issue.

Krishna spoke up to George: "Yes, George. You are made after papa! If they will take care of him, then they will take care of you, too! And even though you are a Lion with different DNA they will take that into consideration and put the mental processes into the works to adapt to your remarkable Lion DNA!"

"They WILL, Krishna? They WILL?" George was excited to ask the question…

"They certainly will, George. *I can see them doing it in my mind!*" Krishna was absolute.

The conversation continued later.

"Let me ask you a question, you Unicorns. Is that okay?" I asked Perle and Peaches the next day.

Perle answered first. She was a much more vociferous creature than Peaches was, even though she was smaller and less robust. "That is a fine way to ask, you hero of heroes! What is your question?"

"Well, you already know what my question is... because you can read minds, right?" I stated. I had a feeling that I already knew the answer to that question.

"Well, yes... we can read minds. But it is plainer to you if you are able to ask the question instead of just listening to answers to random things. Your mind operates in a way that allows for really bizarre thoughts to come into play, that are actual ruminations of science! So, to answer your FIRST question, which is something like this: "What are the elements of science that are predictions of the waves of energy that flow throughout an object that is the product of a Magical effect of the Unicorns?" A tall question, it is! And I have the answer..." Perle paused for a moment and allowed me to add to her statement. And I could tell that she wanted me to add to it...

"So, what is the answer? And is it complicated?" I responded with curiosity.

Perle answered readily: "The waves of Magic are elements that move at the speed of light. That is at the fastest speed that there is within this Universe. Thus, they flow within the blockage of Time that occurs at the highest speeds there is. The reason? Things can't move so fast through time that they can flow faster than the speed of light. They have to move slower in time that ways.

So, there is a condensation between Time and Space in such a way that Time cannot be moving at a speed faster than that of light. But what happens when time is moving backwards? Is it able to do that because it operates at a different frequency than Space does? Does it?"

I answered readily: "That is a really interesting outlook, Perle. How do you process so much information about things that move at the highest speed in the Universe? How do you process it? It seems impossible!"

Perle answered me upright: "It is because I have the Magic power of being able to transit my mind at light speed through the Universe to faraway planets and stars! I have been many different places out there! I have seen things you would think were Magic!"

"Perle. Have you ever seen alien life on other planets?"

"I'm not telling you that! Wait and see what evolution and the Hereafter bring to you!" she said.

I asked her a question that came to mind. "Perle, does the Magic that you see in the Universe play into your assets to make more Magic occur for us people here on this Earth? Do they play a part in it, like in the where-to-fore's of what to do for them? How does it work with there being something called "Magic" within other parts of the Universe? Is it all based on the makings and beings of Nature? Are the Magic procedures all Nature in action?"

"You are a remarkable man! It is a miracle that you are able to write so profoundly about the status of Space and Time the way you do! It is clear that you have an intelligence of 142 IQ, which is in the top 1% of the World! And you used it to write this book! This book should equal the highest Magical Book that has ever been written! What are you going to do if they make a Hwood movie out of your story? What are you going to do THEN? Are you going to write another book? What about your other books? Are you going to act? Are you?" Perle was really carrying on about vaguely related subjects.

"Forget I even write that last paragraph down, reader. I don't want the Hwood producers to use it against me for making this book into a movie. So... never mind!"

Perle was quiet then. She didn't say any more about the subjects. The thing that she had in her mind was about the Magic that she was doing and preparing to do. But she was keeping it secret. She had that capacity to keep things secret. It defied mindreading powers.

But you can read my mind if you try to. Try this... Close the book you have all the way and then think to yourself a question. Any question will do, but preferably something that pertains to the plot of the book. Then ask yourself the question in your mind. Then, asking the question, flip the book to a random page with your finger on a random spot. Read over the word that your finger is on then. The word pertains to the answer to your question! The sentence gives more details into the answer, and the paragraph will answer other relevant questions.

Try it out and see it work! It is a form of Magic! It is the summary of how *information* remains prevalent within the objects brought within Space and Time to us on Earth! What you are reading is *preserved information!* It is linked to your mind, and your mind is linked to my mind as the author though Space and Time with thoughts and writing! Interesting, isn't it?

What is "Magic" defined as? Magic is: "the power of apparently influencing the course of events by using mysterious or supernatural forces." That is what the dictionary online says about the word "Magic". And that is definitely what I mean when I say it. The Unicorns are supernatural forces. And they are mysterious. So, it is within their nature to make things that are Magic in their presence and existence. Take the onsets of Yoga, for example. The structure of the body to move in strange motions throughout the exercise while the person is thinking thoughts of movement the whole time is an element of motion that enables the soul to combine with the body in higher realms of existence. Thus, the exercise of Yoga is supernatural, and it is mysterious in how it enables the body to do such miraculous things. And Krishna was going to be doing Yoga. That was within the minds of the Unicorns for her to do for her wellbeing.

How does one explain the supernatural or the mysterious? By nature, they are things that are meant to defy science and explanation, right? But here I am talking about the Magic things that the Unicorn creatures that I have do. It makes sense to write about them if you really think about it. The reason is because there is something within my character that allows me to take in the mental projections of the Unicorns. That is in part because there have been books written about them. I have one of those books and read it every now and then. I notice them in commercials and on TV shows and in the movies when they are present in them. It seems to me that Unicorns are everywhere, as portrayed by the people who create books and shows and legends. And it is my hope that I will be able to make this book not only a book to read for the eager reader... but also a Legend for the reader to take forwards the story of the Unicorns and how Real Unicorns can operate when in the presence of an Eager for Miracles person!

One of the things that Unicorns are definitely able to do is to read minds and project thoughts to the minds of others. It is like downloading a file from one computer to another. The file screen shows the process of the files being transmitted. Sometimes it shows them one file at a time. Other times it shows the transmission on an icon of multiple files being transmitted at once. Either way, the total realm of the data makes it to the computer... just like the data gets transmitted to the person who is the recipient of the idea being transmitted to him or her. The foundation and the details of the idea come through as the person accepts or rejects the data, like a computer program letting a program through the system. Or rejecting it. A person can do either. Whatever they want to do. It is, after all, their mind that the data is going inside of.

And the data remains secret to the user. The Unicorn has a secret method of transmitting data to others within them, and it transmits to the user the same form of secrecy so that only the user and the Unicorn can tell what the method was that was transmitted. That is a presence of Data Secrecy.

Now I shall write about how the Unicorns are going to use Magic to improve the makings of my health. The Unicorns really want to improve my health, so that I will live a long and prosperous life. They know how to make the parts of the atoms do things that are miraculous! They use their ability to think about the movement of the particles of atoms among each other... the protons and neutrons and electrons... and they have the ability to visualize the Force put forth by the particles throughout their movement. And thus, the Unicorns have the capability of thinking about different Forces and movements and thereby making them do something totally different. Something wholesale in their productivity.

It is thus that the Unicorns have the ability to make matter do things that are crazy. But they work! That is how the Unicorns operate!

What else does Magic pertain to, I wonder? Does it extend to the existence of others? Would it keep someone from committing a terrible incident against me? Could it be set up to give the receiver a mindset of being a Positive Person the does thing that are defined as Good to others, and give them rewards for doing the Good things for me? Is that how it works? I don't know. I just know, from experience, that I would want the Unicorns to put into the mindset of the receiver, or the doer, the onset of Goodness so that bad thoughts would not even be allowed to intervene within their minds. That is what I want. Such a thing would have prevented the bad people from doing such negative things to me that they did. After all, I was a victim of vehicular homicide, and it put me in the hospital for 8 months with brain damage. I recovered, but it took some time.

I recovered. So, what do you think of the book I have written? The Unicorns played a part in that recovery. They helped to bring the molecules of my body and the forces within to a higher level of performance that allowed for them to flow next to each other and deliver excellent causes for remedies within them. The Unicorns did so with mental powers that they have and put forth the thoughts to a Creation of Excellence that defies description.

Thus, that is ALL I HAVE TO SAY ABOUT *THAT*!

"What else are the Unicorns Perle and Peaches going to do to bring us magic? What is on your mind with that question?" I asked that of Krishna.

Krishna responded: "Oh, I don't know. That is a mystical thing, that magic is… what do you think they are going to do with it?"

I answered her with knowledge. "They have told me that they are going to do great things for our health... you and me. That is what they are aiming to do! What parts of that do you think they are going to do?"

"I think they are going to help us to see better." Krishna was saying that because she had gone into the doctor's office the other day and they did a scan on her eye and said that she was bordering on getting blind within a few months. Horrible! They are prescribing eyedrops and medicines to assuage the incident of her getting blind. It may work. It may not. But Krishna wanted the Unicorns to use their miraculous power to keep her from getting blind... if they could do that to her. And today I had seen an eye doctor for a checkup, and he prescribed me a new set of glasses to see better and read better. So, Krishna also wanted the Unicorns to keep me from getting blind, too. Nice of her to do! "You should ask the Unicorns to help it so that you don't go blind!" She knew and was taking into consideration that my diabetes could be an indicator of me going blind before I was that age. So, she was wishing against it, for my well-being.

Then I began to wonder in my mind about what elements of Supernatural events will occur for the Magic to be present. Does "Supernatural" mean that the food within the refrigerator can flow outwards and move itself through space to plates and thereby set itself up on the table? Can atoms of matter flow through space and time to other locations within the body and moving the matter within make the bodies heal more readily? Can the molecules of a guitar get put together within an errant space in such a way that it can operate regularly with divine sound and features about it, and thus be able to operate without anyone really building it outside of thinking with their own mind about it? Are such things possible? Those are Supernatural... right? Can the spirits of objects move and do things that are positive for people who are under the circumspection of magic and miracles? Can they?

They SHOULD they SHOULD.

The becomings of the spirits would be such that they wouldn't be readily seen or known about by the receiver... would they? The one who sensed then would have a sense of Secrecy about them in their mind and wouldn't say much about the supposed sensing of the spirit. The reason is because they wouldn't want to seem insane. And insane is what it would look like if someone expressed that they saw a *spirit* doing things that were far above and beyond regular and normal!

As far as I know, I haven't seen any spirits or ghosts related to the Magic of the Unicorns. But there is a chance that I could have seen them taking on Human Form and making themselves out to seem like they were just normal people! How would a person tell that a person was a spirit if they were just acting like regular people with their bodily appearances and demeanors? There is no way to know! So, there is a chance that I have spoken to Spirits or Ghosts and didn't even know I was! Interesting, isn't it, when you think about it?

There is something about being a former Force Reconnaissance Marine. There is a lot of tactical advantage of the doctrine that takes place as I go through life in general, even though I have gotten out of Force Reconnaissance about 16 years ago. Even more than that, if you consider that I had gone from Force Recon to the MWTC camp that had a lot of regular Marines in it of average intelligence. And I was a smart guy. My intelligence was rated in the top 1% of the world! So, I was surrounded by people with a lesser intelligence than I had, and it interrupted how I performed as an instructor. They tried to teach things that didn't make any sense, because they didn't understand the higher aspects of it, or how to make a rope flow when they were building rope bridges and such. Anyways, my intelligence was interfered with by the stupid people who didn't like it or didn't understand it. I had to deal with a lot of negativities from it. I put my knowledge that I had gained by being a really high performer within the Force Recon platoon doing patrols and anti-terror operations and water exercises in the ocean. I did all those things with excellence, even though many of them were extremely challenging and done in hazardous weather.

The thing is that my intelligence plays a part in how I am treated by Peaches and Perle. They realize that I am capable of seeing the higher aspects of events around me and that I can act appropriately during them without my mind flowing into pieces! The recognize that capability in me and they give me miracles and Magic that moves along those levels of understanding. That is so excellent of them to do that I can't even explain how righteous it is! And it *IS RIGHTEOUS!*

I am employed as an unpublished writer right now. I study mathematics, trying to get back up to the Calculus that I was at 10 years ago. I am reading books on science that are written by physicists and studying Wikipedia websites of higher science topics. I either do those tasks or I write, daily. I barely watch TV. I am trying to figure out Einstein's Relativity, Quantum Theory, M-Theory, the makings of the Universe, and how it applies to the Hereafter after I die. Those all take a lot of thought to persuade a reader to understand them. They are all written about in detail online and in books. It is challenging to read about them on Wikipedia because there are words within the summaries of what is written that describe more detail about it in other pages. And on those other pages there are other words that also have to be looked up. I have opened up six pages to look up terminology for the first paragraph of Quantum Theory. There will be more, I am sure of that.

So, I have the processes of the Unicorns helping me mentally to read over the onsets of the science articles that I am reading. They are also helping me do the mathematics. They are not only doing that, but they are helping me to write about the subject matter by putting descriptive words within my mind in such a manner that I am able to type them into the computer and to make it available for the reader to peruse and take note of. That is a big sentence. I hope I am not writing in to descriptive and detailed a manner for the average reader to understand. I tested at a Genius in the top 1% of the world in the USMC on my SAT test. But I have had brain damage since then, during the vehicular homicide that actually killed me in a coma for a spell. But I have recovered. I don't know what my intelligence is right now, though. I have written a lot of books. The Unicorns help me to make them well written, I think. We'll see how many get published.

Peaches and Perle take alterations of duty in getting involved within my mind when I am writing stories on the computer. They flow within my head and put forth the concepts of detailed and original words to use for the assessment of data with the story. It is words that are high in intelligence and that are heavy in data perused throughout them. Each word has multiple meanings and can be seen in different ways by being surrounded by other seemingly similar words that also have detailed meaning that can be thought about and investigated. They do it quietly, allowing for me to think as though my thoughts are uninterrupted. That helps me to put the words on paper. I am so happy for it, you cannot believe! Then again, maybe you can! It is remarkable what Unicorns are able to do to help a good person! They are remarkable characters!

I have just started to redo my Calculus. It starts out with a person having to know Algebra and Trigonometry. I have even forgotten those and was even having problems with doing basic addition because I haven't done it since dropping out of my Calculus class 10 years ago. So, I have a 10-year period of stalling to make up for. But I am getting the process done, and that is good. The Unicorns help out by helping me to do the processes in the right order in order to get a solid answer. I realize that it is going to take a couple years for me to get my mathematics back up to Calculus 2 – where it was when I dropped out of college – and I had a 96% in Calculus when I dropped out, if I remember right – so I am going to be done with writing this book long before I get done studying the Calculus. But the Unicorns know that, and they are taking heed into the fact of it and treating me accordingly with the learning process.

I'm really wondering what I am going to get out of studying the science and physics aspects of my studies. I want to be the one to determine the Theory of Everything... which hasn't been done yet. There is a lot of data out there, and I do nothing with my time but write and watch TV. I am putting it in my mind to write a lot more now, and to write down more books with a lot more detail. I am also wanting to learn enough about physics to earn a Nobel Peace Prize. That would be so nice! But it would require my intelligence to be near the same 142 IQ SAT test that I had in the USMC, and that may no longer be what it is as. Then again, perhaps the writing has drawn it to that level again. I don't know! But I am going to try.

So, that said, Perle is telling me "Try it! Try it!" in-regards-to studying the Wikipedia files that I have open on my internet connection. So, I shall open up the Wikipedia files and read over some of them, in detail and trying to understand every word that is said. Some of the words are complex words that have deeper meaning. That is within most of the files. So, when I come to one, I must seek out a page regarding it. I have been doing that. The Unicorns help me out with it by helping me ascertain and think about the process behind it. It works out fine!

Ok, I hope this tells you some detail about how the Unicorns work with my detailed and active, but author-based unemployed life. The Unicorns see me as having a lot of potential, and they want to help me succeed with my goals and aims. Their mental preclusions are based on thinking about what a person needs to think to be active and successful. Then they put the successful thoughts forwards with their thoughts through space and time to the mental powers of the recipient... me... and thus Create a forward process of thinking readily. Their minds project thoughts of success and successful thoughts forwards to my mind! They are remarkable Unicorns! Delightful creatures!

I am reading the *Relativity* book by Albert Einstein right now. I just started it. Einstein is supposed to have an IQ of upwards of 160. That is a Genius in the top 0.5% of the World! So, his writing is really detailed in its elegance. The Unicorns are using their Magical abilities to bring me closer to understanding it as I read it. They understand that my math skills are really hurting right now, because I haven't done any Calculus, or any math at all, since I dropped out of college in 2010. This is 2020, some 10 years later. So, I am struggling with doing mathematics. But I have started to do the Algebra again and started on Algebra 1.

The Unicorns are helping me out with it. The mathematics of the remainders of the multiplication decimal problems was put forth by either Peaches or Perle as I was doing it the other day. They were really helpful. I shall get my mathematics up to snuff to do the Quantum Theory and *Relativity* as time progresses. But it is going to be a couple of years... I am sure it is going to be that long, at least. I have been out of study of mathematics for a long ass time. I have to regain my knowledge of it. The Unicorns will help. It is, MAGIC!

That concedes my story about the Magic of the Unicorns and the capabilities of my good friend George the Lion. The story also even has a chapter on the mindsets of Peter the Rabbit and Peter the Lion... two arguably excellent and peaceful characters. The story is about excellent characters that are capable of doing fantastic things. And one may believe that they are "just imaginary". Hah! That defies their capacities as Excellent Creatures! And Excellent Creatures is what they are! How can you not believe in their magical powers?

Now it is time for me to write the final chapter of the book. I hope you enjoyed it readily! My best of wishes to you! And the Magic of the Unicorns is divine upon you as well (if you are a Good person!)

Take it easy!

# CHAPTER 9

## THE FINAL PAGES OF THIS BOOK

This book covers the ins and outs of being a great Lion doll. And he behaves in a rational format that allows for a presence of thought to be around. The question you may have, after reading this story about how George interacts with real people, is this: "Is George actually a doll that is capable of talking to people and thinking about science?"

And the answer will amaze you. The answer is "YES! HE CAN!" He is designed with an output of the capabilities of a Special Operations Capable Unit Force Reconnaissance Marine that is a genius, so George's capabilities are also remarkable! George was designed by Good people who had the oncoming of knowledge of what was occurring with the hero when he was in the Hospital in the coma with brain damage. The Creation of George brought him into the life zone of me and made him capable of repairing and fixing the problems I was having with my health from the incident that killed me for a while in the coma. George is capable of thinking about what elements of thought are possible to make a person heal from injuries, and he has put that capability into fruition.

George has used his connection to other animals (I won't call them "dolls" because they are far more advanced than that description) to get the input necessary to make such healing effects happen. Georges conversations with Peter the Lion and Peter the Rabbit and Perle and Peaches the unicorns is such that it allows for him to make odd-mannered things occur within the molecules and atoms of my body in ways that defy the reaches of common sense. He does so by putting the conversations that he has with those animals into a thought process. Then he takes that thought process forwards and thinks about it in motion with his body to another place, and as he does, he comes up with conclusions based on his reaction to the way his body is moving about. Those conclusions are based on the probability that such thought-action would have a positive effect on the makings of the motions of the particles of the body of the recipient... which is me. Thus, he puts into action a remedy that is effective and well thought out. I really appreciate that.

The story covers that effect, in a way with each chapter. It is mostly about the conversations that me and George and my roommate and friend Krishna had together. They are remarkable conversations. I hope that you enjoyed them. They are real conversations done by George being able to install his thoughts through space and time through the particles of magic to the brain cells of the recipient. That recipient was often Krishna. She would speak for George, in a tone and fluctuation that was different than her normal tone. That was because it was George's voice from his own body coming through her mind to her voice! Interesting how something like that could happen. No such thing has been recorded, as far as I know. But I DO know that there are movies that have been made about Magic and Wizardry that had to come from a period of thought. And the movies were illustrated with periods of Magic occurring. That is an indication that such a thing actually CAN occur... if enough people have thought about it. Perhaps they are using REAL MAGIC at the Hwood Movie Set! Perhaps they are!

The thing is... it is strange how time considers actions and thoughts to persuade a user from processing data in-regards-to the elegant theories. I dropped out of college about 10 years ago. During the time I was in I was getting an A in Calculus class. But I haven't used it since I dropped out. So, that is a 10=year period of my mind being occupied by other things and imprecise thoughts. As a result, I have forgotten even the basics of the mathematics that I need to know to do the Calculus.

That is a loss of Algebra and Trigonometry. I had taken those classes before I went to college and knew them back then. But, because I haven't used them in daily activities, my mind has been interrupted in knowing what they contain as knowledge!

I am attempting to study for Calculus again now. I have to start at the very beginning of the Calculus book to make it happen. And that is not enough, because some of the data is too complicated for me to remember. So, I am having to look up a lot of the information online to get a summary of instructions on how to deal with the data.

But never mind the Calculus book. That is of a nature of being that has little to do with the onset of George the Lion, besides being an avenue of putting mathematics within his capability of being. I understand why a person would think that Calculus is a definition of what occurs with George. People may think that, after all, he is a doll and shouldn't have the special powers that he has! But George is a remarkable creature that does have special powers! And I believe in him, I do I do! So does Krishna!

I am at a loss of where to go now. The structure of the book is finished and is resolute in its performance. It makes me wonder what else a person would want to know about a special Lion that lives like a person does. What else does he say? I don't know. I haven't even written the whole conversations that I had with him down because they were too quick and too long for me to write them down in time for finishing the book. Oh well. The book turned out fine nevertheless and is ready for publishing... as soon as this chapter is done. Granted, I know that there are fewer words in this book than are in the regular sized books put out. Regular sized books are normally 90,000 words long. This book so far, as I write this sentence down, is only 65,065 words long. That is about the size of a juvenile novel. But it IS a story about a doll... so without making things up, what else could I have put in there?

It is challenging to write about a Lion. Especially one that has such a great character. He is able to communicate with me by transferring his speech through the vocal cords of my roommate Krishna. And The word "Krishna" in this case is not of a male. It is of a female. So, I have modified the element of speech too to drive forwards the names of my characters. Thus, the characters are all solid. Granted, they are all made with pseudonyms, for protection against bad things by bad people. There is probably a group of people who think very negatively about the idea of a Lion doing such remarkable things for a Veteran of the USMC. And one that was a member of the Special Operations Capable community, too! That leads to negative thoughts by stupid people who feel threatened by people who are intelligent. I have been a victim of many of those stupid people. There are probably stupid people reading this document right now and taking in this part and getting furious at me for inventing George the Lion. Such people are stupid. George does nothing but the finest things for people. There is no reason for them to hate him. But he IS intelligent. In the top 1% of the world. So, they probably feel threatened by him.

Like I said... they are STUPID.

I don't want to come across as stupid to the reader. The short book may come across as a stupid book made for juveniles. But I think it is written at a much higher level of brightness than that of a "juvenile." I am thinking about writing another chapter on the element of Peter the Rabbit and Peter the Lion and Peaches and Perle the Unicorns. That, I think, would make the book more readable and interject my deep thoughts and imagination into thinking about what those creatures would say to me. I will have to drive Krishna into thinking through their methods of thought for the purpose of transiting the concepts they give to her to me through her speech. She is really good at it. Her mind is open to the concepts of the animals putting forth concepts and ideas to her and speaking them out loud. So, to lengthen this book I think that I shall write an additional chapter along those regards.

Ok, the extra chapter is now done. It is the chapter that leads right up to this one. It is about the Magic of the Unicorns. It is a steady and ready chapter. The book is now, on this word, some 71,185 words long. That is long enough for publishing. For example, there was a book about Wizardry that was a best-seller that was only 77,000 pages long. So, mine is close enough.

I hope you enjoy my book! I have tried to write it as intelligently as possible, with a lot of data and becoming of excellence. That is present, I think! Please enjoy!

That is all! Take good care of yourself, your friends, your family, your roommates, your boyfriend or girlfriend, or total strangers that you meet. Take good care of all of them! And best of luck to you, and my blessings upon you, the reader!

# BIOGRAPHY OF MITCHELL KRAUTANT

Krautant, Mitchell (2020). California, USA. IngramSpark.com

Mitchell Krautant is a genius who tested with a 142 IQ when he was in the USMC. He served in SOC Force Recon there. He departed the Marines injured. Then he went to prison when he was innocent. They were highly illegal there and the prison staff gave him PTSD. He got sent to mind bending solitary confinement, which placed him under severe mental duress for 7 years after he was released.

When he was released, he went to college and was getting an A in calculus 2. But the mental trauma of solitary confinement overwhelmed him, so he dropped out of college and became homeless.

Mr. Krautant went homeless to the VA hospital and received no care there. He departed and was a victim of vehicular homicide. He died in the coma and was taken to the Hereafter by three of God's Angels. After he came back to life, he became an author.

He has written the *Cheetah on the Wing 1-4* books, *Movement to the Hereafter, Death and Life as a Victim of Vehicular Homicide,* and *The Elegant Lion Named George.*

There are even other books to follow!


www.mkrautant.com